MATANZA

The 1932 "slaughter"
that traumatized a nation,
shaping US-Salvadoran policy
to this day

THOMAS P. ANDERSON

CURBSTONE PRESS

Second EDITION, 1992
Originally published by the
    University of Nebraska Press
Copyright © 1971 by the
    University of Nebraska Press

Cover design by Les Kanturek
Printed in the U.S. by Princeton University Press

Curbstone Press is a 501(c)(3) nonprofit literary arts organization
whose operations are supported in part by private donations and by
grants from the ADCO Foundation, the Connecticut Commission on
the Arts, the Lila Wallace-Reader's Digest Literary Publishers Marketing
Development Program administered by CLMP, the LEF Foundation, the
Andrew W. Mellon Foundation, the National Endowment for the Arts,
and the Plumsock Fund.

Library of Congress Cataloging-in-Publication Data

Anderson, Thomas P., 1934-
     Matanza / Thomas P. Anderson — 2nd ed.
          p. cm.
     Includes bibliographical references and index.
     ISBN 1-880684-04-7
     1. El Salvador — History — 1838-1944. 2. Communism — El Salvador.
I. Title.
F1487.5.A67 1992
972.8405 — dc20   92-24610

distributed in the U.S.
by InBook
P.O. Box 120261
East Haven, CT 06512

CURBSTONE PRESS
321 Jackson Street, Willimantic, CT 06226

for Ian Anderson

Contents

Preface to the Second Edition

It has now been twenty years since the publication of *Matanza*. It has been in print almost continuously since that time and was published in Spanish by EDUCA, Costa Rica. From this it might be gathered that the book struck a responsive chord, but this is probably not due to the book itself so much as to the dramatic events which unfolded over the last two decades in El Salvador. In this brief space I should like first to say a few words about the book, and then something on the subsequent events of Salvadorean history.

It is the nightmare of every historical writer that some sharp scholar will find fatal flaws in his work that will prove that he was either a fraud or a fool, but *Matanza* appears to have largely stood the test of time. Indeed, it is disconcerting, especially as you grow older, to be frequently told that your first book was your best. However Professor Kenneth J. Grieb did point out in his review in *The Americas* that I had overlooked certain State Department files that proved that Jefferson Caffery was actually trying to remove Martínez from power (p.62). I suppose I was fooled by the opposite impression he gave the Salvadoreans, as well as by having overlooked certain files.

I have also been called to task for calling it a "communist revolt" in the title. This matter was brought up at a symposium on the book at Universidad Centroamericana in San Salvador some years ago and more recently at a New York University conference. I believe that I did emphasize the Indian element in the uprising and the peasants' general discontent, but there is no denying that the revolt was led by men such as Agustín Farabundo Martí who were indeed communists, and while the revolt came prematurely, they were planning an uprising. Therefore, there are three elements to the revolt, indigenous resentment of the *ladinos*, more generalized peasant resistance to oppression, and communist leadership.

Lastly, there is the matter of the body count. At the UCA Symposium, my low figure of eight to ten thousand *campesinos* killed was also questioned. Many people claim more, but a friend of mine, who was born in Santa Ana and lived in the area of the revolt most of his life, pointed out that, if such a vast number of people were killed, they ought to find remains all over the place, but they don't.

As for El Salvador itself, my impression when I first went there for research in 1969 was that the country desperately needed a revolution. The outrageous poverty, the arrogance of the wealthy, the ubiquitous armed repression all seemed to point to revolution. I have not changed my mind. The memory of 1932 for a long time frightened the populace into docility. Then things began to change, the fraudulent election of 1972, when José Napoleón Duarte was robbed of the presidency appears to have been a turning point. Peaceful change, always the hope of many, now seemed no longer possible. Armed Marxist insurgent groups began to appear. Thanks, to liberation theology, much of the Catholic Church joined the opposition to the regime and many priests and nuns were martyred. In October, 1979, a junior officers' coup toppled the Party of National Conciliation, but the military repression and the death squads continued, and the pallid reforms that the junta led by Napoleón Duarte undertook did not satisfy the revolutionaries. The result would be more than a decade of civil war between the Farabundo Martí Front of National Liberation and the government.

Despite their many mistakes, the revolutionaries could have, indeed should have, won in early 1984 when they were at the peak of their power, but their revolution was not convenient for United States foreign policy during the Cold War, and the result was massive aid to the government which succeeded in producing the current stalemate.

Today, in the four fifths of the country under government control, a situation curiously like that of pre-1930 El Salvador prevails. Alfredo Cristiani of the right-wing ARENA party presides over a liberal government (in the nineteenth century sense) run by and for the entrepreneurial elite.

Unions are repressed, sometimes by violence and the modest land and banking reforms of the late President Duarte are annulled while the death squads are given free rein. But the modern business elite has a partner the old Fourteen Families would have shunned: the office class. Bloated by the war and incredible amounts of United States aid, the military has become a major business institution. The senior commanders may not know how to beat the insurgents, but they certainly know how to turn a buck.

The situation is volatile, peace negotiations are continuing, but, for the moment, El Salvador seems to have come full circle, and, aside from the increased role of the military institutions, be where it was before the election of Arturo Araujo. So much was hoped for in 1930, so much became tragedy. One can only hope that sometime soon El Salvador can waken from its reoccurring nightmares.

Thomas P. Anderson
Eastern Connecticut State University
October, 1991

Preface

This study was born out of curiosity about the communist revolt of 1932 in El Salvador, an event which has frequently been mentioned in studies of communism in Latin America, but never explained in detail. In an effort to find additional information on the subject, I approached a number of scholars in the general area, including historians Rollie Poppino and Neill Macaulay and sociologist Richard N. Adams. They had nothing further on the revolt, but thought that the subject seemed worth looking into.

Accordingly, I began searching for material on the event. I applied for a grant from the Social Science Research Council, which was kind enough to accede to my request, and with this money I was able to spend some months in El Salvador interviewing knowledgeable persons and checking other sources of information. The government of El Salvador insisted that it had nothing further to release on the rebellion, but I was fortunate to come in contact with a number of persons who had material on the revolt. The documents of Col. Osmín Aguirre y Salinas were especially helpful, as were unpublished accounts lent to me by Miguel Pinto, Jr., Alejandro D. Marroquín, and others.

A number of other persons aided me in my researches. Among these were Lynn Beck of Agricultural Extension; Father Fausto Cristales of Nahuizalco; Dr. David Luna of the University of El Salvador; Apolinas Meneses Carías of Agricultural Extension; Juan Norio, a journalist and labor organizer; Andrew J. Ogilvie, a North American student of history; Gustavo Pineda of *Diario de Hoy*; Ernesto Sol Trujillo, an engineer of San Salvador; and especially, Leonel Gómez Vides, a coffee grower from Santa Ana. In addition, the staff of the National Library of El Salvador, the Library of Miguel Angel Gallardo, *Diario Latino*, and *La Prensa Gráfica* were most helpful.

Chapter 1

The Political and Social Background

It was as if nature had gone mad. All of the northern portion of Central America had been set rocking when Volcán de Fuego, Volcán de Agua, Acatenango, and several lesser craters in Guatemala all erupted at once on the night of January 22, 1932. Not to be left out, the "lighthouse of the Pacific," El Salvador's famous volcano Izalco, joined in. A cloud of ashes blanketed the skies as far away as Nicaragua. The population of western El Salvador, the heart of the volcano region, was in terror. Molten lava began to drift down the slopes of Izalco, and those who lived near the mountain began to pack hastily, for Izalco was noted for its destructive rampages.

And then, in the glow of the burning mountain, a more ominous development was observed. Bands of Indians armed with machetes were making their way out of the ravines and tangled hills down into the towns of the area. In their eyes burned the bright light of fanatic determination. Before dawn came on the twenty-third all of the western part of the country was aflame, not with molten lava, but with revolt. The peasants had chosen the moment of Izalco's eruption to launch one of the bloodiest revolts in the history of Latin America. Before this revolt was ended untold thousands would lose their lives, unspeakable outrages would be committed, the nation's economy would be set back for years, and the entire personality of the nation of El Salvador would be changed.

The revolt was no mere *jacquerie*, no sudden impulse on the part of Indian *campesinos*. It was, on the contrary, the result of a long chain of events both within the country of El Salvador and outside it. Further, it has the distinction of being the first Latin American revolutionary movement in which men who were avowed international communists played a major part.[1] It marks, therefore, the beginning of a significant new phase in the history of the region. The age of ideologies had come to Latin America. Why the communists chose El Salvador for their debut in the Western Hemisphere, how the revolt of 1932 came about, and what were its causes and aftereffects are questions which must be answered in detail to be answered at all, for the roots of this revolution are many and complex. To begin with, it is necessary to know something of the state which calls itself after the Savior of the World.

In many ways, El Salvador fits the stereotyped idea that most North Americans have of Latin American countries. It is small, roughly the size of New Jersey. It is densely populated, squeezing some three and a half million persons onto its surface at the present time, or a population of better than two hundred persons per square mile. It is lacking in mineral resources, warm in climate, and studded with volcanos. Most of its people live in unsanitary poverty, but it supports an extremely wealthy aristocracy. It is a one-crop country, still largely dominated by the coffee-producing interests. It has a tradition of coups d'etat and military rule. It has, in short, almost everything that the average reader in the United States would think of as "Latin American." It appears to be a typical banana republic, except, of course, that it does not export bananas.

In actuality, however, El Salvador is an atypical Latin American state. It is the smallest mainland republic in Latin America, and the only one in Central America that does not face both oceans. It is the most densely populated state, not only in Central America, but in all of continental Latin America. Further, when one searches its history more closely one easily discovers that its historical pattern only superficially resembles that of its Latin neighbors. El Salvador is unique, a land apart, as its natives and its friends proudly boast, and nothing sets it apart so much as the story of its past.

1. Robert J. Alexander, *Communism in Latin America* (New Brunswick, NJ: Rutgers University Press, 1957), p 336. For reasons which will become clear in the course of this study I cannot classify the revolt as purely communist, but it is undeniable that communists played a large part in it.

It has been said that happy countries have no history. It is equally true that chronically unhappy countries have a monotonous history of strife and turmoil, and El Salvador is a chronically unhappy land. Its foundation was the result of the exploits of that famous and barbarous conquistador, Pedro de Alvarado, who marched south from Mexico to conquer the Central American region for Spain in 1524. Alvarado was, in addition to being a most capable administrator and general, a cruel and vicious despot who crushed the Indians of the area and reduced them to vassals of the crown.

The Indians whom Alvarado found in the area of modern El Salvador were of several highly civilized stocks. In western El Salvador, south of the Lempa River, the original inhabitants appear to have been Mayan. However, around the time of the Spanish conquest and partly in conjunction with that conquest, Nahuatl-speaking Indians, related to the Aztecs, moved into the region and displaced or absorbed the earlier groups. Central El Salvador continued to be inhabited by Maya related groups.[2] Both these groups of Indians had been in a semicivilized state when the Spaniards arrived. There was already a division of labor; there were already large estates worked by a multitude of willing, or perhaps not so willing, hands. What the Spaniard added was not so much the economic exploitation of the Indian peasant, which had been pretty well advanced under native rulers, but rather the element of cultural shock. Whatever the merits of Indian society, all within it were united by common religious, cultural, and ethnic traits. When the Spaniard came he substituted an alien hierarchy, totally out of contact with the masses, which tried to reproduce medieval Spain in modern America.

On the surface Spain succeeded to a surprising degree. The Indian was Christianized, forced to submit to Spanish law and customs, and even protected to a certain extent by these laws and customs from the Spanish colonist. The Indian was fitted into the Spanish economy. Through the tribute system of the

2. Gordon F. Ekholm and Gordon R. Willey, eds., *Handbook of Middle American Indians: IV, Archaeological Frontiers and External Connections* (Austin, Texas: University of Texas Press, 1966), pp. 134, 153-55, 210-13.

encomienda and through the *repartimiento*, a kind of Spanish corvée or forced labor, he was made to work for his new masters. *Encomienda* and *repartimiento* were in time replaced by a system of debt slavery, but each of these systems mercilessly exploited the Indians and contributed to a decline of their numbers, as even Spanish writers are forced to admit.[3] And although the Indian was blended in economically, even intermarriage, or more accurately, interbreeding, failed to bring those who thought of themselves as Spaniards into real contact with those who still considered themselves Indians.

During the period of Spanish rule, El Salvador was a colonial backwater. It formed a part of the Captaincy General of Guatemala. San Salvador, the chief town of the ill-defined region, was not even the seat of a bishop. Communications were slow throughout Spanish America, and news generally reached San Salvador late, if at all. Nonetheless, several citizens of the area played an important role in the independence movement at the beginning of the nineteenth century. In 1811 a creole aristocrat, Manuel José Arce, and his uncle, the priest José Matías Delgado, led an abortive revolt against Spanish rule. The revolt was crushed, the ring leaders were imprisoned, and stern measures were taken to prevent a new outbreak.

But when Mexico declared her independence from Spain, there was no longer any way by which Spain could maintain her hold on Central America. In 1822 Iturbide of Mexico attempted to incorporate the Captaincy General of Guatemala into his newly formed Mexican Empire, but within a year Iturbide's empire was no more, and the general he had sent to subdue Central America shrugged his shoulders, changed sides, and began to instruct the people in the art of setting up their own state. Arce, the Salvadoreño, became the first president of the Federal Republic of Central America, which had its seat of government, at that moment, in Guatemala City. Arce was unable to hold the quarrelsome Central American provinces together, but his successor, Francisco Morazán of Honduras, had

3. For instance, see Julio Alberto Domínguez Sosa, *Ensayo histórico sobre las tribus Nonualcas y su caudillo Anastasio Aquino* (San Salvador, 1964), p. 32.

better luck for a while. Morazán became president of Central America in 1830. He twice invaded El Salvador to quell separatist movements. As long as he held the key region of Guatemala he could keep the union together, but Rafael Carrera, an illiterate Indian muleteer, led a peasant uprising against the Central American Republic in Guatemala.

Carrera, a bloodthirsty and ignorant butcher, had the backing of the church in Guatemala because the clergy opposed the liberal regime of Morazán. Morazán failed to defeat Carrera and lost control of Guatemala as a result. In 1834 the capital of what was left of the state of Central America was moved to San Salvador. After that disintegration slowly set in. Morazán held out until 1839, when he abandoned control of El Salvador and resigned as president of Central America. With his resignation the reality of a Central American union came to an end.

But the dream lingered on, especially in El Salvador. In fact, much of the political history of the country can best be understood in terms of this never forgotten ideal of unity which, ironically enough, has plunged El Salvador into war with her neighbors time and again. Even the recent war with Honduras in the summer of 1969, a war which divided Central America more deeply than ever before, had its roots in the attempt to create a Central American common market which was vigorously sponsored by El Salvador.

Another recurring theme in the history of El Salvador is that of intervention from Guatemala. Guatemala enjoys better communications with El Salvador than does any other state, and throughout much of their history Guatemala has given the lead to its smaller neighbor. Politically speaking, when Guatemala sneezes El Salvador catches cold. This was first demonstrated in 1839 when Carrera, then the dictator of Guatemala, installed his own appointee as president of the new Republic of El Salvador. His choice was Francisco Malespín, an extremely conservative militarist. Malespín was murdered in 1846, and a number of troubled years followed. The ablest man during this period was the liberal leader Gerardo Barrios, a corpulent, goateed general who became president in 1859 and attempted to restore

Morazán's Central America. Unfortunately, all that he succeeded in doing was to plunge the whole of Central America into turmoil and civil war. Finally Rafael Carrera invaded El Salvador again, deposed Barrios, and again substituted a man of his own, Francisco Dueñas, a member of one of El Salvador's most famous families. Barrios, however, refused to let well enough alone. From exile he attempted a comeback in 1865, was captured in Nicaragua, shipped home to El Salvador, and executed. In that same year Carrera died, but he had succeeded in establishing conservative rule not only in Guatemala but throughout most of Central America. With the death of Gerardo Barrios and Carrera the "formative years" of Central America came to an end, those years which Mario Rodriguez has characterized as "a violent period of ideological struggles and unadorned selfishness."[4]

They were also years which saw the beginning of profound economic change. During the colonial era a satisfactory diversified economy had been developed, based on maize and other food crops along with "balsam of Peru," indigo, tobacco, cacao, and other tropical products. It was a lazy economy which brought little money into the country. This economy survived independence, but it could not survive in the world of the Industrial Revolution. The Spaniard had given the Indian a bad case of cultural shock. Now it was the Creoles' turn to be shocked out of their economic apathy when they looked about them in the middle of the nineteenth century and saw a world in which they were increasingly unsuited to compete, a world of railways and steamships, of industrialization, specialization, and concentrated production. The exploits of the filibuster William Walker, and of the economic filibuster Commodore Vanderbilt, in Nicaragua and Honduras, gave the Central American states a warning during the 1850s. Either they must come to terms with the modern economic world or become colonies of those who had.

The Central Americans came to terms in the only way they could. They chose to enter the world market, and El Salvador's

---

4. Mario Rodríguez, *Central America* (Englewood Cliffs, N.J.: Prentice-Hall, 1965), p. 92.

passport turned out to be coffee. Costa Rica was the first to begin the large-scale Central American production of this crop in the 1830s, and in the sixties, under the enlightened leadership of Gerardo Barrios, El Salvador followed suit.[5] Coffee caused an economic upheaval. Coffee was a cash crop. You cannot eat coffee. It has to be processed by the *beneficio*, or coffee-drying plant, to be used at all. You can only exchange it for money and then buy what is needed. Thus, the multicrop economy was replaced by what gradually became a one-crop, cash economy.

The death of Gerardo Barrios was followed by a period of political as well as economic change. During the next quarter of a century there were no less than six new constitutions. For the most part the liberal faction, noted chiefly for their anticlericalism, was in control, the chief reason being that a fellow "liberal," Justo Rufino Barrios, had taken control in Guatemala and imposed *his* views upon his smaller neighbor. Justo Rufino Barrios was a tough-minded dictator who took his cue from Porfirio Díaz of Mexico and his "positivist" regime of state sponsored capitalism. Like Mexico and Guatemala, El Salvador prospered during the decades of the seventies and eighties, or to be more accurate, some Salvadoreños prospered greatly, while the masses of the people sank further into peonage.

Justo Rufino Barrios became unhappy with his own hand-picked president of El Salvador, Rafael Zaldívar, and in 1885 he invaded El Salvador with the intention of showing him where God lived. Unfortunately for the Guatemalans, a stray bullet ended the career of Justo Rufino Barrios in the very first battle, and his army fled in a rout back to Guatemala. Zaldívar then resigned in favor of Francisco Menéndez, a "popular and enlightened man"[6] who drafted the new constitution of 1886, a document which was destined to last until 1939. Menéndez, one of the abler presidents of the country, was overthrown in 1890. There followed a period of coups and short-lived regimes which came to an end in 1903 when a system for regulating the

5. Ibid., p. 102.
6. Thomas L. Karnes, *The Failure of Union: Central America, 1824-1960* (Chapel Hill, N.C.: University of North Carolina Press, 1961), p 166.

presidential succession came into effect. By this system the president in power picked a candidate to succeed him and this official candidate was then duly elected in an election replete with all the trappings of democracy: opposition candidates, political platforms, and balloting. Of course, the outcome of these elections was never in doubt, but they did prevent the violent and often bloody overthrows which had until then been common.

During the nineties, El Salvador had been bitten once again by the unification bug. An attempt to create a "Greater Republic of Central America" was made, but it broke down in 1898 and the turn of the century witnessed a complicated struggle among Nicaragua, Guatemala, and El Salvador, in which the last-named appeared again as the champion of unification.

Despite the official-candidate system for choosing the president, there were still vicious political contests in the country. These political rivalries were not based on rival programs but rather on the personalities of contending caudillos.[7] In 1912 these passions led to the assassination of President Manuel Enrique Araujo. Upon his death a man by the name of Carlos Meléndez became president. He dutifully finished Araujo's term, then engineered his own election and served from 1915 to 1919. Further, he founded a political dynasty that carried on after him. He was succeeded first by his brother, Jorge Meléndez, from 1919 to 1923, and then by Carlos's brother-in-law, Alfonso Quiñónez Molina, who served from 1923 to 1927.

One good thing about the Meléndez-Quiñónez period, as it is called in El Salvador, was the absence of coups. But the reason for this was that the presidents were thorough-going dictators who ruled with an iron hand on behalf of a conservative aristocracy and the military.[8] Their rule was aided no doubt by the presence of an equally conservative regime in

7. Alberto de Mestas, *El Salvador: País de lagos y volcanos* (Madrid, 1950), p. 492.
8. F.D. Parker, *The Central American Republics* (London: Royal Institute of International Affairs, 1964), p. 151.

Guatemala during most of this period. Under the Meléndez-Quiñónez dynasty, political repression of the *campesinos* and the fledgling working class helped sow the seeds of the 1932 rebellion.

However, to succeed himself in office, as he was allowed by the constitution to have only one term, Quiñónez picked Don Pío Romero Bosque who was in office from 1927 to 1931. Don Pío, as he is always called, is remembered in the mythology of his country as a kind of Salvadorean Good King Wenceslaus. In later years men were to look back on the period of the beloved Don Pío as a golden age in the country's troubled history. Romero Bosque was an economic and social conservative who, as we shall see, alternately tried to conciliate and to repress the masses, but he was startlingly able, and even more startlingly honest. He quickly cut himself off from his unsavory predecessors and attempted to clean up Salvadorean politics. He managed to shunt aside the members of the dynasty, even forcing Dr. Quiñónez into exile, and when his period in office was drawing to an end, instead of following the time-honored customs of Salvadorean democracy, Pío Romero Bosque decided to hold a free and democratic election. It was destined to be the first, and for a long time to come, the last such election in the history of El Salvador.

To understand the reasons for the failure of Romero Bosque's experiment in democracy, we will have to turn to the social and economic conditions of the country during the period from the first Meléndez to the election of 1931. Part of the reason for the boldness of Don Pío in breaking with the Meléndez-Quiñónez group was the unparalleled economic prosperity at the start of his presidency. The fact was that there had been a dramatic rise in the coffee economy since Carlos Meléndez's election in 1915. The value of coffee exports had risen from $7,372,000 in that year to $22,741,000 in 1928. The amount of land in coffee production in 1928 was half again as great as the amount in production in 1918. Despite the fact that many deplored the social consequences of this growth, especially as more and more of the coffee lands became concentrated in the hands of the elite, it appeared that coffee prosperity was here to stay.[9]

Then came 1929. Even before the great crash, coffee prices had started downward. With the start of 1930 this downward trend grew markedly worse and most producers preferred to let the harvest of 1930 rot in the fields. The country became permeated with the sick-sweet smell of rotting coffee fruits. As many of the *fincas*, or coffee plantations, were heavily mortgaged, the owners often lost their land. Some 28 percent of the coffee holdings in the country changed hands during the early years of the depression, the small growers generally suffering more than the large.[10]

The debacle focused the attention of critics on the growing dependence of the economy on coffee, which was accused of not only strangling the economy but also of creating social chaos and the impoverishment of the masses. Mario Zapata, one of the young revolutionaries of 1932, pointed out in an interview given in the last days before his execution that coffee had been responsible for the destruction of the country. Before the age of coffee El Salvador had a balanced economy of grain, fruit, and other crops, "but then came the age of coffee and everything changed....The ambition to make more money obliged the capitalists to search for greater extensions of land for coffee plants....If a small landholder refused to sell, the rich man, the coffee man, went to the local or departmental *comandante*."[11]

9. Everett A. Wilson, "The Crisis of National Integration in El Salvador, 1919-1935" (Ph.D. diss., Stanford University, 1970), pp. 44, 132, 285.
10. Alejandro D. Marroquín, "Estudio sobre a crisis de los años treinta en El Salvador" (Unpublished essay), pp. 21-23, 48. Coffee production during the depression (except for 1931, for which no data exists) ran around 1,300,000 quintales of 46 kg each. Land under coffee cultivation was about 100,000 hectares.
11. Rodolfo Buezo, *Sangre de hermanos* (Havana, n.d.) pp. 17-19. This book claims to give the memoires of the revolutionary Mario Zapata as received second-hand from a Salvadorean official. The accuracy of the work is questionable, but if these were not Zapata's exact words, they probably represent his thoughts. Buezo was the secretary to Alfredo Schlesinger, a rabidly anticommunist Guatemalan journalist. Schlesinger was given most of the papers of the government of El Salvador concerning the revolt. These were used by Buezo and also by Alfredo's son Jorge in writing their respective books. Popular legend in El Salvador has it that Alfredo

On the other hand, Abel Cuenca, a rebel leader who survived the revolt of 1932, points out in his thoughtful book on the socioeconomic structure of the country that coffee was at first a progressive force. Coffee did not institute the plantation economy: quite the opposite, as Cuenca demonstrates. Plantations for the growth of maize, cattle, and fruit had long existed. Coffee had to struggle against the existing agricultural system in which the peon, tied to the land and his *patrón,* was the chief worker, because coffee required thousands and thousands of seasonal workers, who would not be tied for life to the *finca* but would come and go with the harvest season of November to February. Further, coffee cannot be blamed for immediately seizing lands which had originally raised cereals. Coffee at first took the highlands where little else grew. Only as coffee prices increased during the twentieth century did the monster come down from the mountain and begin to gobble up the plain.[12] In all, coffee made possible great advances during the period around the turn of the century and the following two decades.

But coffee became, inevitably, a vested interest. Behind the changes of presidents there grew an unseen government of the coffee growers. These men guided politics to suit themselves and their interests, just as the old manorial landholders had done before them. The Asociación Cafetalera became a second state. "If low salaries were an important requisite...their policy consisted in keeping salaries low,...and if this meant that manufacturing must vegetate due to a lack of an internal market," then that was what would have to happen, for nothing could interfere with coffee.[13]

Coffee also created a class of super wealth consisting of men whose wealth was not simply in land, but was received in hard cash from the sale of coffee in Germany and the United

Schlesinger became angry when General Martínez refused to pay him for writing a progovernment version of the 1932 revolt and sold the documents he had received to the Russian government. I have not been able to verify the authenticity of this story.
12. Abel Cuenca, *El Salvador: Una democracia cafetalera* (San Salvador, Mimeograph edition: n.d.), p. 17.
13. Ibid., p. 30.

States. The descendants of the powerful coffee families tended to marry foreigners; they were educated abroad, and in time became almost a new race, differing from the rest of the Salvadorean nation not only in social mores and prejudices, but even in color and other physical characteristics. Coffee had "opened a profound chasm in the Salvadorean collectivity."[14] This new race is often referred to as the "cosmopolitan upper class," and is characterized as being part of an international social elite. During the thirties the newspapers were full of stories of their long, slow steamship rides to Europe. Today they would be part of the jet set. In the early decades of the century, as today, these people tended to live in the large cities, especially San Salvador. Below them there has always been a class of local aristocrats, made up of prosperous landholders who divide their time between their estates and their residence in the chief regional towns. These two classes are referred to collectively as la sociedad or gente de primera categoría.[15]

It would be wrong to imagine that this is a completely frivolous aristocracy, especially today. These people, educated in North American or European universities, supply the engineers, medical doctors, economists, and scientists so desperately needed in an emerging economy. Still, during the early decades of the century, the existence of this group tended to be parasitic. The young women were purely decorative and given chiefly to gossip. The young men, the señoritos, as they were derisively called, spent most of their time playing pool or dominoes, or with their lower-class mistresses, while waiting for their fathers to die so that they could inherit the family estates. Even if they had wanted to engage in hard work, family tradition limited them to a few professions, chiefly law.

Below the upper classes exist a local middle class of small business owners, craftsmen, and minor landholders. These people have traditionally lived without ostentation, but fairly well. Below them is the overwhelming majority of the poor.

14. Jorge Schlesinger, Revolución communista (Guatemala, 1946), pp. 16-17.
15. Richard N. Adams, Cultural Surveys of Panama, Nicaragua, Guatemala, El Salvador, and Honduras (Washington: Pan American Sanitary Bureau, 1957), pp. 462-63.

These divisions are perhaps too simple. Cuenca divides Salvadorean society into no fewer than eleven social classes: the *latifundistas, colonos, terratenientes,* urban proletariat, small farmers, minuscule proprietors, the important commercial class, shopkeepers, industrialists, white collar workers, and artisans. In his system, the *latifundistas* are the owners of lands which produce grain, cattle, or fruit. These lands are worked by *colonos,* or farm hands. The owners of the *latifundios,* traditional masters of the country, have found their society and power breaking down over the last fifty years because of the rise of the *terratenientes,* who are the masters of the great coffee plantations. These lands are worked by seasonal agricultural labor, or semipermanent field hands, who live on the *fincas.*[16]

Both *latifundista* and *terrateniente* have to live off the labor of the masses. Coffee, especially, is a crop which requires many hands, during the November-to-February harvest and at other times, such as when trees are being planted. Some of the labor, as pointed out above, is done by persons who live on the *finca* as *colonos.* These people are defined as salaried farm hands who are given a place to live on the estate and a *milpa,* or garden plot, plus a small wage, and in return are to provide an ever ready source of labor. On the *latifundios,* where work is more regular, they make up the bulk of the work force. But on the coffee plantations they are supplemented by harvest labor which is recruited chiefly from the miniscule proprietors. This gives rise to a rather interesting paradox. El Salvador is a land of large estates, and at the same time a land in which almost all the rural population either own some land or have it leased to them from the big estate owners. In 1950, for instance, a careful survey showed that out of 174,204 land exploitations in El Salvador, 33,398, or 19.2 percent, were *milpas* for *colonos.*[17]

16. Cuenca, *Democracia cafetalera,* pp. 13-16. *Terrateniente,* literally meaning landholder, is used technically. The cotton producer is also a *terrateniente* to Cuenca. Notice that here people are being classified by their relationship to the "means of production," while in Adams's work they are classified by life style.
17. Adams, *Cultural Surveys,* pp 431-35. Of the holdings under 7.5 acres, 25 percent were *colonos'* garden plots. As this 25 percent would be 32,426

Further, it can be seen that there was one land exploitation for about every fifteen persons in the country. Even aside from the *milpas*, the majority of these land exploitations have always been very small. A few hundred families have some 80 percent of the land.

Now it should be obvious that the conditions of the *colonos* and seasonal workers varied from time to time and place to place. As in manorial Europe or the Old South, there were good masters and bad masters, but the general consensus seems to be that the lot of the rural worker was generally pretty bad. In his novel *Ola Roja*, Machón Vilanova gives a picture of the life of a *colono* family around 1930. "The majordomo of this *finca* was a rude and authoritarian man who made Matías and the boys work all week for an insignificant salary and took from their pay at the end of the week a peso from each for the rent on the hovel where they lived. The rest of the salary was not given in real money but in tokens which could only be used to buy food, clothing, medicines and trinkets which the wife of the master bought and left in charge of the wife of the majordomo."[18]

The great crash made the life of the rural poor infinitely worse. During the depression the value of the colón fell from 2.04 to the dollar in 1929 to 2.54 to the dollar in 1932. The national income by 1931 sank to 50 percent of what it had been in 1928. *Campesino* wages, which had run around fifty centavos a day before the depression, sank to twenty centavos a day, when there was work to be had at all. It is perhaps fortunate that food prices also fell steeply during this period, corn dropping to half its 1928 value by 1932, rice to about 75 percent of its 1928 value, and beans to little more than half their predepression cost.[19] This did not help those who raised these crops for sale, however, and the net result must have been to reduce the *campesinos* to the subsistence level.

The depression accentuated certain curious facts of Salvadorean rural life. Because of the seasonal nature of much

plots, and the total number of *milpas* was 33,398, it can be seen that the average *milpa* was very small.

18. Francisco Machon Vilanova, *Ola Roja* (Mexico, 1948), p. 295.

19. Marroquín, *Crisis*, pp. 13, 19, 23, 34. [Jorge Arias Gómez], *Biografía de Agustín Farabundo Martí* (San Salvador, 1967), p. 18.

of the work, and because the *colono* also frequently changed masters, or drifted off to the cities in search of a better way of life, there was, and still is, a great mobility among the rural poor of El Salvador. One result of this mobility has been a breakdown of the family structure. It is a well documented fact that most of the unions of man and woman in the country are extramarital, and more than half the births are illegitimate. Barón Castro, in his demographic survey, says that in 1935 there were 59.5 illegitimate births out of every 100.[20]This situation appears to have been especially bad in the western part of the country, the area in which the rebellion of 1932 took place. A survey as late as 1950 found that in the three westernmost departments, Sonsonate, Santa Ana, and Ahuachapán, one-third of the population lived in common-law unions and only 18 percent were married.[21]

How does it happen that in a nominally Catholic country such a high rate of illegitimacy and concubinage could exist? Some consider that the expense of a wedding fiesta might be part of the answer. Further, it could be due to the fact that marriage under Catholic law is indissoluble. An obvious explanation lies in the life style of the Salvadorean poor. Given the marginal conditions of life of the rural worker, the frequent necessity of pulling up stakes and moving to another part of the country, and the general added expense of living with a wife and children, it is not surprising that in many cases a man, forced to go about in search of work, takes up the handiest woman he can find. He lives with her for a while, supports all the previous children she might have had by other itinerants, and then, when the boss gets too overbearing or the coffee is harvested, he moves on. The woman, saddled with an ever increasing brood, stays put, waiting from some other worker to come along and give her temporary support.

20. Rodolfo Barón Castro, *La población de El Salvador: Estudio acerca de su desvolvimiento desde la época prehispánica hasta nuestros días* (Madrid, 1942), p. 542.
21. Adams, *Cultural Surveys*, pp, 457-58. The survey goes on to note that one-third of all urban and one-fifth of all rural households are without a male head.

In the rich coffee-growing region around Santa Tecla, I recently saw miles of cardboard shacks, mostly refrigerator cartons, which served as home for a large number of people. A coffee planter told me that during the spring and summer these pasteboard towns are inhabited exclusively by women and children, waiting for the harvest, when men will come who will, hopefully, support them for a time and not beat them too much. He assured me that this was the long-standing custom of the region.

Marriage, after all, is a going institution because it is an economically feasible one. When it ceases to be economically possible, then all the Sunday sermons in the world will not induce people to legitimize the birth of their children. The priests in El Salvador, who are often few and far between, try their best. Local pastors often declare that anyone over twenty-one who is not married is in a state of mortal sin. But in El Salvador, as in Venezuela and many other places in Latin America, people tend to feel that it is better to be in a state of sin than a state of bondage. All this, of course, holds good only for the lower classes, and beginning at the level of the local middle class where inheritance of property is important, the institution of marriage is as stable in El Salvador as anywhere in the world, although keeping mistresses is also very common.

Considering these facts, one is not surprised that the country grew in population during the early twentieth century despite the lack of marriages. By 1930 there were 1,459,578 people in the country, of whom 48.69 percent were males. For statistical purposes 39.5 percent of this population was classified as "urban," but that simply meant those living in any towns. Actually, there were no cities to speak of other than the capital, and that had only around 80,000 souls. A more reasonable estimate gives the rural population as 80 percent.[22] Since 1930 the population has not only more than doubled, but it has also shifted in distribution. In the early twentieth century the population was concentrated in the western and central part of the country. In 1930, 340,176 inhabitants lived in the three

22. Marroquín, Crisis, p. 14. The official statistics can be found in the Anuario estadístico de 1930 (San Salvador, 1931).

westernmost departments, and 710,621 in the seven central departments.[23] Since that time the population has tended to drift eastward.

One demographic question of considerable importance, but which is very difficult to answer, is what percentage of the population considered themselves Indians. When one asks today of a sophisticated Salvadorean how many Indians there are in the country he will probably answer, "That is a false question. There are no pure Indians here. Almost all of us are part Indian in race but there are no real Indians left." But this answer evades a very real problem, especially in regard to the 1932 revolt. It is certainly true that almost everyone in El Salvador has Indian blood. Barón Castro, in his exhaustive and monumental study of the population of El Salvador, estimates that as late as 1940, 20 percent of the population were of pure Indian extraction, while 75 percent were of mixed Indian and white blood and only 5 percent were true *blancos*.[24]

But in El Salvador, as elsewhere in the region, it is very difficult to determine who is an Indian. Perhaps the best method is to say that an Indian is as an Indian does. That is to say that those who follow Indian customs are Indians. Sociologists list a number of customs which distinguish Indians from Ladinos, as those who follow Spanish ways are often called. One sign of an Indian is linguistic, the survival of his Indian dialect; another is political, the survival of distinct Indian political organizations, generally headed by a cacique; in the area of religion, sociologists note the existence of separate, Indian *cofradías*, or religious brotherhoods. Miscellaneous Indian characteristics include distinctive dress, especially for the women; living in grass, thatched-roof huts; and handicraft industries. In a few places, such as Izalco in the heart of the area of the 1932 uprising, the people exhibit many of these

23. José Tomás Calderón, "Población-tierra-trabajo," *Revista del Ateneo de El Salvador* 135 (1932): 8-10. For the growth of the capital city since 1930, see David R. Raynolds, *Rapid Development in Small Economies: The example of El Salvador* (New York, Washington and London: Praeger Inc., 1967), p. 7. San Salvador did not overtake Santa Ana as the largest city until the early years of the present century.
24. Barón Castro, *Población*, p. 527.

traits even today. In other locales, such as neighboring Nahuizalco or distant Panchimalco, some Indian traits are still in evidence.

In talking to the Indians of the western region I found none who still, in 1969, spoke Nahuatl as their first language, and only a few older people who could say a few sentences for me. The most distinctive features in evidence were in women's dress, with the long, wraparound, flower-print skirts coming down to the ankle, and (as I discovered somewhat to my embarrassment) the custom that many Indian women have of going topless at home in their grass huts. *Cofradías* are still strong organizations.

Basically then, an Indian is one who thinks of himself as an Indian and is so regarded by others. Given this definition, a survey of 1950 found about 400,000 persons who could be regarded as Indians in El Salvador, a figure which, considering the increase in population, tallies pretty well with Barón Castro's estimate of 20 percent. However, the Salvadorean census of 1930 claims that there were but 4,051 Indians in the department of Santa Ana, or 2.6 percent of the population; 20,572, or 26.1 percent, in Ahuachapán; 34,764, or 34.7 percent, in Sonsonate; and 8,749, or 5.9 percent, in La Libertad province. This same census listed only 79,573 Indians in the entire country, or 5.6 percent. But it is clear that the criteria must have been different from those used in 1950.[25] In any case, it seems clear that those who could be regarded as Indians were concentrated in the western part of the country.

Most Salvadoreans would deny that the Indian is regarded as a cultural inferior, and this may be true today, for the number of those who are culturally Indians has so declined in the last decade as to make the species as rare as the North American Indian, and therefore people who should be preserved as part of "our cultural heritage." However, abundant evidence exists to prove that this was not the feeling in 1932; cultural antagonisms played a large part in the 1932 revolt. Moreover, the Indian himself carried a smoldering resentment against the Ladino which went all the way back to the time of Alvarado. The Indians never fully accepted Spanish rule, and

25. The 1950 figures are from Adams, *Cultural Surveys*, p. 489.

"around their fagot fires on chilly nights the old Indians narrated the history of the early days, tragic and sombre scenes of violent persecution, mixed with heroism and deeds of unrecorded glory....In the hearts of the conquered race arose sentiments of hatred and vengeance."[26]

In 1833 an Indian by the name of Anastasio Aquino, who lived at Santiago Nonualco, in the south-central part of the country, led a revolt against white rule. After massacring the Ladino settlements near his home he marched with an army of thousands of ill-armed Indians against the whites at San Vicente. Aquino's revolt was caused by the anarchy of the early independence period, and by the fact that the situation of the Indian was progressively growing worse. Independence had meant the end of whatever slim protection the crown afforded him and he was at the mercy of a creole aristocracy which believed in freedom for themselves only. Aquino marched into San Vicente, and seizing a crown from the statue of Saint Joseph, put it on his own head. However he was decisively beaten there and hanged by the government. His followers were punished and dispersed.[27]

J. Hugo Granadino, the distinguished Sonsonate historian, sees in the 1932 outbreak definite overtones of race war, while "Quino Caso," the well-known Salvadorean writer, told me that he felt the revolt was definitely related to Anastasio Aquino's revolt of almost exactly a century before.[28]

There is little doubt that the hostility was mutual. In the novel *Ola Roja* the hero protests that in 1931 there are some twenty-five thousand people around Sonsonate without enough to eat. A lawyer answers, "Those 25,000 are miserable Indians who content themselves with a salary of four *reales* a day, which is what their indolence is worth, and their ignorance and laziness....

---

26. Jorge Schlesinger, *Revolución comunista*, p. 17. See also Lilly de Jongh Osborne, *Four keys to El Salvador* (New York: Funk, Inc. 1956), pp. 28-29.
27. Domínguez Sosa, *Anastasio Aquino*, pp. 83-84.
28. I must add that many equally well informed persons disagree. Abel Cuenca, when I interviewed him in 1969, told me that there was no Indian-Ladino split in Tacuba where he led the revolt. But Tacuba was not within the belt of Indian towns around Izalco. For information on these and other interviews, see sources at the end of this work.

I did all that was possible to better the conditions of the Indians, but didn't accomplish much because of their lack of cooperation....They speak our language in school, but on leaving revert to Nahuatl."[29]

Understandably, after the revolt of 1932 the feeling of Ladino towards Indian was very bitter indeed. A Ladino survivor from Juayúa, interviewed a few days after the revolt, said, "We'd like this race of the plague to be exterminated....It is necessary for the government to use a strong hand. They did it right in North America, having done with them by shooting them in the first place before they could impede the progress of the nation. They killed the Indians because they will never be pacified. Here we are, treating them like part of the family, and you see the result! They have fierce instincts."[30]

An article in *La Prensa*, February 4, 1932, was entitled: "The Indian has been, is and will be the enemy of the Ladino." The author, a landholder from around Santa Ana, wrote that "there was not an Indian who was not afflicted with devastating communism....We committed a grave error in making them citizens." Yet these same people depended on Indians to work their estates and had Indian servants in their homes. It was an interesting aspect of the revolt of 1932 that houseboys and personal servants were often among the leaders. Even in a survey written in 1935 for the purpose of improving the educational opportunities of the western Indians we find the author saying that the Indians are "given to sexual vices, are carriers of venereal diseases and are alcoholics."[31]

Not all the hostility came from a mutual distaste for the personal habits of the other group. The Indians, as noted above, were left at the mercy of the Ladino aristocracy at the time of

29. Machon Vilanova, *Ola Roja*, pp. 30-31.
30. Joaquín Méndez, Jr., *Los sucesos comunistas en El Salvador* (San Salvador, 1932), p. 105. This book is an invaluable series of interviews taken by Méndez, an able reporter, only a week or two after the events.
31. Adolfo Herrera Vega, *El Indio occidental de El Salvador y su incorporación social por la escuela* (Izalco, El Salvador, 1935), p. 71. The author adds, "In the *cofradía* he drinks too much, becomes criminal, exchanges wives" (Ibid., p. 75). It is curious that this book, printed in Izalco, only three years after the revolt took place, never once refers to these events. However, it is obvious that they are very much on the author's mind.

independence. After the middle of the century the aristocracy was guided by principles of private enterprise which dictated that the communal farming system of the western Indians must be destroyed. The town lands, or *ejidos*, were broken up, as in Mexico, starting in the sixties. Many of the poorer Indians then found themselves with insufficient land for subsistence. This led to an Indian uprising at Izalco in 1872 which was severely repressed by the government. While not as significant in size as the revolt of Anastasio Aquino, it played its part in confirming Indian-Ladino hostility.

Even though many Indians had been forced to become *colonos*, many residents of the Izalco area insist that at the time of the 1932 revolt "the Indians were better off than the Ladinos," and that "most of them owned their own land." It appears to be true that a good many had managed to retain or to buy back some small plot, but the Indian community was largely dependent on part-time work on the *fincas*.

The 1932 revolt, of course, caused strong measures to be taken against Indian culture. There was a noticeable drop in the number of persons adhering to Indian dress, customs, or language after 1932.[32] This was due in large measure to the great massacre, but as time went on the chief impetus to change appears to have been the desire to slough off the characteristics of a despised group within the population. A Salvadorean Indian could cease to be one by moving "a few kilometers," as one of them put it, adapting "western" dress for his wife, and taking care to speak reasonably good Spanish.

In so far as the Indian of the pre-1932 period had a separate political and social identity, this identity could be summed up in two words, *cacique* and *cofradía*. The cacique, or chief, of the Indian community was not an official of the Ladino government. He was an extralegal authority who owed his status to his recognition as the leading figure among the Indians of his town or district. He might coexist alongside the town governmental structure and be on good terms with the *alcalde* and other government officials. He did not owe his post to any particular role in the religious societies or *cofradías*, though he

32. Adams, *Cultural Surveys*, p. 504.

was generally an important figure in one or more of these. Rather he was a kind of "mayor of China Town," who could be appealed to in order to keep peace among the Indians or to influence their voting in elections. His authority was vast but indefinite, and varied from place to place according to his own personality.

The most important of the caciques was a leader of the town of Izalco, which was and is in large part an Indian town. It actually consists of two "towns," or *barrios*, an upper and a lower one. The upper town (north and farther up the slopes of Izalco Volcano) is called Barrio Dolores and is Ladino town. The south town, lying along the Sonsonate-San Salvador road, is called Asunción and is Indian town, although many Ladinos live there. Each of these areas has its own church and plaza. Of the 5,966 persons living in Izalco in 1950, 75 percent were Indians by cultural definition. Of 16,289 rural inhabitants 25 percent were cultural Indians.[33] Over the Indian population the cacique exercised a considerable authority before 1932, representing his people before the government and using their power as a voting block to influence elections. No other Indian leader in El Salvador had the power of the cacique of Izalco, nor enjoyed equal recognition from the official government. After 1932 this recognition was largely withdrawn. Government officials insist today that there is no cacique of Izalco. However, Félix Turish is universally regarded as holder of that title by all the Indians to whom I spoke in 1969. In 1932 the caciques of Izalco and Nahuizalco took a significant part in the revolt.

Many other leaders derived their position of leadership not from being chiefs but rather from their positions within the *cofradías*, which were an important aspect of Indian Catholicism. The chiefs of these organizations had, in fact, tended to usurp the authority of the caciques. Like the latter, they were able to get out the Indian vote, and therefore often had their vanity tickled by astute politicos.[34]

These Indian societies differed in some ways from other Catholic associations which might be formed by Ladinos. One

33. Ibid., p. 486.
34. Jorge Schlesinger, *Revolución comunista*, p. 11.

point of difference was the survival of an Indian outlook toward religion. Catholicism in Central America had not completely exterminated pagan ideas, and in many cases it was difficult to tell where Indian Catholicism left off and Indian paganism began. The *cofradías* were, and are, devoted to the worship of a single saint or person of the Trinity, whose name they bore. There was a Cofradía de Jesús a Gatas, a Cofradía de los Siete Dolores, a Cofradía de Espíritu Santo, and innumerable others. In 1932 the most powerful was that of Espíritu Santo, whose leader was Feliciano Ama, cacique of Izalco. These societies differed from Ladino organizations not so much in the extent of their superstitions, but rather in the nature of their beliefs and practices, many of which derived from remote, pre-Christian sources. Sometimes the groups were the bane of the Catholic clergy. The current pastor of Asunción tells me that he has never been allowed to witness the ceremonies of the local *cofradía*, which is presumably a parish organization. Each *cofradía* supported its own fiesta and religious observances through a system of voluntary contributions and through the voluntary cultivation of the *tierra del santo*, land belonging to the religious group, or of a portion of an individual member's land set aside for that purpose. The "saint" himself, in his statue or painting, lived in the *casa de cofradía*, a house in which the ceremonies of the organization were held.[35]

These religious societies had a definite political role in the pre-1932 period, and it was through them that "advanced ideas" such as communism filtered through to the Indian masses in the Izalco region. The regular clergy, on the other hand, tended to preach resignation and the acceptance of the status quo.

While the question of Indian versus white folkways was of considerable importance in the Izalco-Nahuizalco area, its significance decreased as the distance from that region increased. In Tacuba, Ahuachapán, and other far western areas, in Soyapango just east of the capital, and in the Colón-Santa

---

35. Adams, *Cultural Surveys*, p. 495. The same book states on p. 475 that these organizations include women as well as men. It may be that the charge of immoral behavior comes from this fact, as the Spanish mind would prefer segregation of the sexes.

Tecla region just west of the capital, the factor of cultural conflict was not important, and yet the revolt of 1932 occurred in all these areas. What was true, throughout most of rural El Salvador, was that there was a profound gap between the *campesino*, especially the *colono* or the transitory *finca* worker, and the wealthy and middle-class citizens. Even where all were Ladinos, the peasant tended to be looked down on as part of a distinct caste. Immediately after the 1932 revolt Francisco Osegueda delivered a radio address which was reprinted in the *Revista del Ateneo* for 1932. He compared the *campesino* who had just revolted against his masters with the "*campesino* of old," who "although unlettered...loved God, respected the rights of others, idolized the family, was cooperative." But "inflamed by cheap, popular orators," the *campesino* of today "invades the cities with a heart full of venom, dizzy with his own selfish desires. He is without any notion of what is truly human, ignorant of the rights of others."[36]

In an essay written some years after the revolt, another Salvadorean writer made similar observations. Declaring that communism was infiltrating the *campesinos* and making them discontent with their lot, he went on to say "the truth is the workers, the *campesinos*, don't deserve the good life. And the reason is that they do not do anything for themselves, they don't strive, don't accept responsibility or save. This attitude is always destructive of the state, because the shiftless individual always looks for someone to blame and charge with his own sins."[37] There is a certain obvious similarity here to the nostalgia of some North American whites for the good old darkie who knew his place and never asked for his rights.

When one combines all the reasons for peasant discontent—the breakdown of the *ejidos*, the miserable treatment of *colonos* and hired hands, the social problems and dislocation caused by the coffee economy, the cultural hostility between Indian and Ladino, and the class hostility between

36. Francisco R. Osegueda, "Observaciones sobre la vida del campesino salvadoreño de otros tiemos y la del campesino actual," *Revista del Ateneo de El Salvador* 135 (1932): 11-15.
37. Roger Mendieta Alfaro, *¿Democracía o comunismo?* (San Salvador, n.d. [1952?]), p. 191.

campesino and landholder—and then, when one adds to this the economic disaster of the depression, it is not hard to see the basis of the revolt of 1932. That some movement would arise that would seek to harness this discontent and provoke a rebellion was almost inevitable; that the movement would be communism was a fact dictated by events which began with the Russian Revolution and which were part of a pattern in which El Salvador was an insignificant piece.

Chapter 2

The Rise of the Left

For all of the nineteenth century and for the first two decades of the twentieth, Latin American labor, both agricultural and urban, was a formless mass, a putty that the wealthy landholder or businessman could manipulate as he saw fit. Government generally conspired with business interests to make the organization of either peasant or industrial workers impossible. The *guardia*, and similar paramilitary police organizations, were the handmaidens of agricultural capitalism. But the apparent triumph of labor in Europe and North America could not but affect the situation of the working classes in Latin America. Thus it was that, spurred by the examples of the Mexican and then the Russian revolutions, laboring masses all over Central and South America began to unite and demand basic rights. Given the violent nature of revolution in Mexico and Russia, it was understandable that this awakening took a radical and violent form, and that it was a political as well as an economic awakening.

The first steps toward popular organization in El Salvador were taken with the formation of Liga Roja in 1917. Although ostensibly a labor organization, the league was deeply political in purpose, and while it appeared from its title to be a first cousin of the Bolshevik party, it was in fact a means of manipulating the lower classes for the benefit of the old crowd already in power. The organization was the brain child of Dr. Alfonso Quiñónez Molina, a clever medical man from Suchitoto, who became the brother-in-law of President Carlos Meléndez. The Red League had a red flag for its banner, vague socialist sentiments for its program, and much more important, an armed militia of its own which operated with the blessings of the government. Local chieftains of the Red League could offer their followers virtual immunity from arrest for political crimes, and common crimes as well. Through its votes and strong-arm methods, the organization helped to elect Carlos's brother Jorge Meléndez in 1919, despite his being a very unsavory politico with no record as a friend of labor. Then, in 1923, it was used to propel brother-in-law Quiñónez Molina personally into office.[1]

During the latter's election campaign, the league committed some nasty excesses of zeal. On Christmas Day women demonstrating in favor of Dr. Miguel Tomás Molina were massacred in the streets of San Salvador. By that time the politicos had begun to feel that the league had served its purposes anyway. There was, after all, always the danger that this curious example of Salvadorean Zubatovism, in which the state became the leader of the revolution, might deviate from its projected course when the agricultural workers who made up the bulk of the organization's membership discovered there was nothing for them in cooperation and decided to turn on their masters. It is hardly surprising then that Quiñónez Molina, safely in office, harassed the officials of the league, broke up its meetings, and eventually smashed its organization.

During the twenties, more genuine labor organizations began to spring up in Central America. These groups had very little basic industry from which to draw support. Their urban contingents were recruited from skilled trades such as printing, from service industries, and from transportation. As time went on, they discovered that they could not hope to survive without also including the peasants. Around 1922 the first steps were taken toward the establishment of a unified labor movement embracing all of the Central American republics, and in 1926 the Confederación Obrera Centroamericana, called COCA for short, was established.

In El Salvador, the first labor unions got started in 1923. The next year they formed the Federación Regional de

---

1. [Arias Gómez], *Marti*, pp. 6-7. David Alejandro Luna, "Un heroico y trágico suceso de nuestra historia," in *El proceso político centroamericano* (San Salvador, 1964), pp. 49-50.

Trabajadores de El Salvador, the FRTS. This organization linked itself to COCA as did Guatemalan and Honduran groups, each of which was called Federación Obrera. The movement had its headquarters in Guatemala City.

Although the name of COCA sounded very impressive, the realities were anything but inspiring. The organization was poor in numbers, weak in organization, and completely incapable of carrying on a real workers' movement. It claimed, however, to speak for Central American labor, and outsiders were inclined to take this claim at face value. Many of those associated with COCA were international socialists, and not a few were communists, but COCA was at first quite moderate in its ideas. As time went on, it became increasingly militant and its activities played a part in bringing on the 1932 uprising.

After the Federación Panamericana de Trabajadores emerged as a United States-backed effort to sidetrack Latin American labor from its socialist tendencies, COCA began to manifest more openly its left wing character. In May, 1929, the Salvadorean FRTS and the other Central American syndicalist groups sent delegates to the founding of the Confederación Sindical Latino Americana, which came into being in Montevideo. After this date, the importance of the regional organization COCA declined considerably, and it virtually went out of business. Its functions as a regional organization were merged with the *confederación*. Both organizations had their share of Marxist socialists, many of them Moscow-oriented communists.[2]

It was not only by means of the Confederación Sindical that leftist ideas were being spread. The Anti-Imperialist League, founded in Guatemala in 1927, was also strongly communist in outlook, especially in the Salvadorean branch, which quickly gained considerable strength.[3] This organization, as its name might indicate, specialized in anti-North American activities. Relations between the United States and its southern neighbors were very poor during the twenties. Intervention in Nicaragua, Haiti, and the Dominican Republic had soured a good many

2. Alexander, *Communism*, pp. 366-67.
3. Ibid. As Alexander notes, the league especially attracted intellectuals.

Latin Americans on Uncle Sam, and the Anti-Imperialist League, while it might have had the blessings of the communists, had little difficulty in whipping up enthusiasm for reasons which had little to do with Marxist ideology.

In addition to these various organizations, there was a small Communist party working underground in El Salvador from about 1925. It had been founded by organizers from Guatemala and Mexico. The party did not really begin widespread activity until 1930, when the Mexican agitator Jorge Fernández Anaya appeared on the scene. He was a communist of long standing who had organized the Aztec Farm Workers Union in Mexico. Along with a number of subordinates, Fernández Anaya toured El Salvador in the spring of 1930, hitting especially the western zone and concentrating on the farm workers. Of marked Indian features and speaking Nahuatl, he managed to blend into the countryside and the authorities were unable to catch him. Dr. David A. Luna states that Fernández Anaya and his followers managed to organize eight thousand workers in three months, which, if true, would make it one of the most miraculous mass conversions since Pentecost. On May Day, 1930, the communists staged an eighty thousand-man parade through the streets of San Salvador. Official announcement of the party's foundation had come in March.[4]

Until 1929, the communist organization in El Salvador had been directed by the Guatemalan party council, but in 1929 a Secretariat of the Caribbean was formed, with its headquarters in New York. After the official foundation of the party in El Salvador, the Salvadorean communists took their orders from New York. As far as the internal direction of the party is concerned, by 1930 there was a Central Executive Committee in San Salvador. Next in the chain of command came the Departmental Executive Committees, and below them were the Comités Ejecutivos Locales Regionales. At the bottom was the customary cellular structure. Each cell was made up of about five to twenty individuals. The dues for the individual were a modest six centavos a month, plus a ten-centavo initiation fee.

4. Luna, "Trágico suceso," p. 55. Mauricio de la Selva, "El Salvador: Tres décadas de lucha," *Cuadernos Americanos* 21 (January-February 1962): 198.

These dues were divided, with 50 percent going to the Central Executive Committee in the capital and 25 percent going to the Departmental Executive Committee. The local party kept the remainder and it is safe to say that if the dues represented the total party income, very few party leaders were likely to be living in grand style.[5] It is possible that small amounts came from outside El Salvador.

From the highly organized party structure, one might draw a false picture of tight discipline and careful organization. The reality was much less formidable. The party was never the great, sinister organization that it was later made out to be by the government of General Martínez. In many places only a paper organization existed.

Probably the most flourishing radical group in El Salvador, and certainly the wealthiest, was not the Communist party, but rather the closely allied Socorro Rojo Internacional. This "red aid" society had one of its more important chapters in little El Salvador, thanks in large part to the genius of its local leader, Agustín Farabundo Martí. Good communists were instructed that they were supposed to be members of the SRI as well as the Anti-Imperialist League.

SRI was often referred to as the "Red Cross of Communism," but its functions went beyond mere emergency care and hospital work. A propaganda leaflet put out by the organization describes it as follows:

> The SRI is a vast organization, without party affiliation, which accepts the idea of class struggle. It proposes to defend all the workers who are persecuted by imperialism, capitalist governments, and all other agencies of oppression,...proportioning its legal aid and material and moral support to those workers and their families by means of agitation and publicity and organized demonstrations....The aid of SRI is also extended to the families of the persecuted and the fallen in the revolutionary struggle....All persons, whatever their

5. Jorge Schlesinger, *Revolución comunista*, pp. 123-28.

politics, race or nationality, who fill in the card of admission and are in accord with the ends of the organization, promising to fulfill the statutes, have a right to be considered as members in good standing of SRI.[6]

The claim to be above party was not exactly true, although the majority of members in the organization were probably not communists. Certainly, the ties between the Communist party and the SRI were very close, and Martí, the director of SRI, was in fact the unofficial leader of all Salvadorean communists.

Although the material aid that SRI could render was important, its emphasis was on propaganda, especially that kind of propaganda which could embarrass the government into releasing political prisoners. Martí, as we shall see, had this down to a fine art. To carry on its work, SRI drew on dues, but it also received some funds from New York, where the international organization had its headquarters. A government-seized document dated October 14, 1930, was sent from the group in New York to the Salvadorean branch of the organization. In it the New York group, called the SRI Secretariat of the Caribbean, asks for information about expenses incurred in organizing, in disseminating propaganda, and in giving aid to prisoners. Since the document concludes by asking how much the Salvadorean section would like to receive monthly, there were presumably some funds available.[7] In addition to its links with the Communist party, SRI maintained close ties with the Anti-Imperialist League, and protests started by the SRI were often taken over by the league.

Another league, this one begun by the SRI, was the Liga Pro-Luchadores Perseguidos. The organization grew out of recommendations made at the sixth congress of the FRTS and

6. Photo of document in Gustavo Pineda, "La Tragedia comunista de 1932," *Diario de Hoy*, January 18, 1967. This is part of an interesting series of articles by Señor Pineda and his associates which were published from January through March, 1967, in the San Salvador daily.
7. Photo of document in Jorge Schlesinger, *Revolución comunista*, p. 207. This document is signed Jorge A. Vivo and is addressed to "Octavio Figueira."

was implemented through the SRI. The *liga* was set up by Víctor M. Angulo, who became secretary general. Other officers in this arm of the proletarian struggle were Tomás Coto Gonzáles, the organizational secretary; Juan A. Guardado, the propaganda secretary; and Rafael Bondanza, financial secretary.[8] Only the last named was a prominent communist chief. Bondanza became the right-hand man of Agustín Farabundo Martí, and played a prominent part in the 1932 rising, after which he was captured and shot.

The growing prominence of an international Marxist group in El Salvador caused considerable problems for the growing FRTS. By 1930 this labor organization numbered some fifteen hundred members, mostly among shoemakers, carpenters, and bakers in the departments of San Salvador, Santa Ana, and La Libertad. The original leaders of the *federación* had been more attracted to anarcho-syndicalism than to communism, but before long the communists were making determined efforts to seize the movement and give it a new and more realistic direction. In January, 1930, a definite break occurred between the syndicalists and the communists, with the latter gaining control of the greater number of local chapters.

To the communists it was quite clear that only through the organization of the farm workers could socialism expect to triumph in a country which was still mostly rural. This might have been heresy in Moscow, but Moscow had largely ignored the seemingly insignificant parties in the Caribbean, and the independent-minded leaders in El Salvador were practical enough to see that only a *campesino*-based union had any chance of mass support. By April, 1930, the new masters of FRTS were able to gain fifty thousand signatures to a petition demanding a "workers' law" that would guarantee farm contracts and set a minimum pay for agricultural workers.[9] May Day, 1930, saw a massive turnout of eighty thousand workers and peasants. This demonstration was followed by a series of marches and protests, most notably on June 18, demanding that the president open unemployment centers in each city.

8. Ibid., p. 84.
9. De la Selva, "Lucha," p. 198.

All this unrest has to be seen against the background of the Great Depression. When the people of the capital city marched on the president's house, as we are told in the *Diario del Salvador* of July 1, 1930, they shouted, "We demand work; we have no way to live," and this was literally true. Hunger and hopelessness had been endemic even before 1929 for the vast majority of the *campesinos* and urban poor. The depression had pushed them over the line between dumb submission and desperate fury.

Certainly, without the catastrophic fall of coffee prices, the prolonged crisis of 1930 to 1932 which led to the great rebellion would never have come about, but the form in which the crisis was handled by the militant Marxists indicates that they had done a great deal of preparatory work. The activities of Jorge Fernández Anaya, the Mexican Marxist leader, have already been mentioned. But he was no "voice crying in the wilderness." Indeed, he was more of a Saint Paul than a John the Baptist, a latecomer who found the field already well prepared for his work.

The Marxist sentiments harbored by so many Salvadoreños in the time of Don Pío Romero Bosque owed their existence to a number of men, both natives of El Salvador and foreigners, who had worked for this cause over a number of years. These men, who received little aid from the international Marxist movement and who labored in great poverty and often in danger, had disseminated the ideology of the left to the peasants and workers of El Salvador. Often, like Fernández Anaya, they worked as laborers; many of them were seized, imprisoned, even tortured or killed by the police and the *terratenientes*. But always some of them managed to go on spreading the message of revolt and class struggle. These precursors would finally achieve their goal of converting the poor into a militant force, only to see that force vanquished in 1932. Among the early militants who paved the way for the '32 revolt were such men as Esteban Pavletich, Juan Pablo Wainwright, Modesto Ramírez, Luis Felipe Recinos, Miguel Mármol, José Luis Barrientos, and Agustín Farabundo Martí. In their various histories one can see some of the strange paths taken by Latin American radicalism.

In 1920, as a result of the unsuccessful agitation against the right wing dictatorship of Peru, a number of radical students were expelled from the country. Among them was a young Peruvian of Yugoslav descent who bore the unlikely name of Esteban Pavletich. Undismayed by his exile, Pavletich bummed around Latin America and in a little while managed to set himself up as a student in Guatemala, where, in appearance at least, he was little different from the rest of the crowd of footloose students sent abroad by their wealthy families. He next turned up in Cuba, where he became a friend of the radical leader Mella, who was killed in Mexico a short time later. Pavletich himself went to Mexico where he lived for three years, and it was there that he met Agustín Farabundo Martí and other left-wing leaders from El Salvador. Like Martí, he went into Nicaragua where the patriot leader Augusto Sandino was locked in combat with the United States Marines, sent to keep a more conservative government in power. At various times Pavletich entered El Salvador.

Pedro Geoffroy Rivas has told me that he remembers being with Pavletich at a meeting in 1929, when Pavletich and Haya de la Torre came to explain to the FRTS the principles of Alianza Popular Revolucionaria Americana (APRA), the radical Peruvian organization which intended to beat the communists at their own game by proposing a dynamic social program based not only on international socialism but also upon appeal to Indo-American loyalties. Alfonso Luna, who was to play a tragic role in the 1932 massacre, attended these meetings.

Pavletich was an unceasing and untiring agitator, and a methodical organizer and propagandist. He was no communist, but rather he resembled in character the young Russian Nihilists who had "gone to the people" in the 1870s. Jorge Schlesinger says of him: "Instructed, and blessed with great intellectual powers, along with iron will and an extreme fanaticism for his creed, he stood out among a crowd of agitators."[10]

The last time we find him in El Salvador is in July, 1930. On July 13 the newspapers carried the story that he had been discovered living in the country under the name of Esteban

10. Jorge Schlesinger, *Revolución comunista*, pp. 24, 42-44.

Trujillo after being expelled from Mexico for what the newspapers called "communist activities." Evidently he returned to Peru shortly afterwards, was again exiled, and returned once more before being permanently exiled to Chile.

A character at least as colorful was Juan Pablo Wainwright, born in Santa Barbara, Honduras, the son of an English father and a Honduran mother. Like Pavletich, he left home while still a youth. Wainwright traveled to the United States and became a tramp, drifting back and forth across the nation. He was a fisherman in Alaska, a dishwasher in San Francisco. There he was accused of stealing thirty dollars, and fled toward Mexico but was brought back and tried. Found guilty, he was placed on probation, subsequently enlisting in the Canadian army during the First World War. He evidently had a good war record and was promoted to sergeant. After the war he became a sailor and drifter again, but eventually married and settled down in his native Honduras.

His views were too radical, however, for him to be able to live very long in that country. He fled to El Salvador in the twenties. After a time he was expelled for his subversive activities but took up residence in Guatemala. From Guatemala, he coordinated plans for a great Central American revolt, working with Martí in Salvador. However, *Diario Latino* (San Salvador) announced on January 15, 1932, that Wainwright and a large number of followers were captured the day before in Guatemala by Ubico's government. This capture may have been related to Martí capture four days later, and may have been an important factor in the decision of the Salvadorean leaders to bring on an early revolt.

Imprisoned and put to the torture, Wainwright volunteered to give a "sensational revelation," but only to the dictator Jorge Ubico in person. Ubico came to the prison and demanded the news.

"The news is that you are a dirty, murderous human beast," said Juan Pablo Wainwright, and he spat in the dictator's face. Thereupon he was beaten to death by Ubico's torturers.[11]

11. Ibid., pp. 44-46.

Such men as Wainwright and Pavletich were international agitators, men educated by travel and experience. Other leading recruits came from more humble origins. Modesto Ramírez (who survived the 1932 debacle long enough to be interviewed by Alfredo Schlesinger, a right-wing Guatemalan newsman) was a peasant of Soyapango, El Salvador, who did not know how to read or write. "I had been an honorable laborer," he told Schlesinger, "living on the haciendas that surrounded Lake Ilopango as a *colono* of various señores. There came a time when we were not given land or work, or if there was land, it was of the worst quality." If the men were lucky enough to find a position they were forced to give more than half their produce to the *patrón*. Those who objected were expelled. "I had to abandon my wife and children. I did not get enough work to be able to give them food, still less clothing, or to educate them. I do not know where they are. Misery has separated us forever.... For this I became a communist."

Ramírez became attached to a group of communists centered around Miguel Mármol, a shoemaker by trade. As a member of the working class, the radical militant Mármol was more effective even than Martí in talking with members of that class. He was to be a major leader in the 1932 revolt. In 1930, Ramírez took a trip to Russia with Miguel Mármol, passing through Guatemala to Puerto Barrios and then embarking for Hamburg. "There we were received by an English comrade who spoke perfect Spanish and who put us on a train for Leningrad where we joined our comrades Antonio Sánchez Obando and Juan Luis Chigüichón of Guatemala and the Honduran delegate, Hernán Anaya," he told Schlesinger. These men were given tours of Leningrad and Moscow, if Schlesinger's account can be trusted, and were permitted to witness the maneuvers of the Red Army, "which defends the rights of the proletariat against capitalists and the bourgeoisie."

Even when the Salvadorean revolt failed, the convictions formed by this journey remained with Ramírez. "I believe," he said, "that the power will be ours and our children's, because there are many of us. In the world there are more communists than enemies of our cause,...I know that there are more poor than rich and all who suffer hunger and want are on our side....They are going to kill me? No matter, it will be my fate like that of my comrades. I prefer it to suffering as I have."[12]

Among the Salvadoreans most responsible for the creation of a proletarian consciousness among the poor were Luis Felipe Recinos and José Luis Barrientos, neither of whom was a communist. As a university student of just seventeen, Recinos was expelled from Salvador in 1920 because of his advanced views. He settled in Mexico where the reform movement of Alvaro Obregón was just getting under way. There he took a job with the Pro-Obregón newspaper, *Lucha*. Perhaps at the time of Obregón's assassination, Recinos crossed into the United States, where his travels opened his eyes to the possibilities of an organized labor movement. Although still attracted to Marxist ideas, he became a reformer rather than a radical. On his return to Central America he took up journalism once more and became one of the outstanding practitioners of that art in El Salvador, working for Miguel Pinto's *Diario Latino*. He was one of the chief figures behind the organization of the FRTS, and also behind the successful candidacy of Arturo Araujo, in 1931, for the presidency.[13] Although Araujo found it necessary to repudiate him during the campaign, he was later given government positions in the brief period of Labor party rule— among them, ironically enough, the position of chief censor of the press after a state of emergency had been proclaimed. He fled with Arturo Araujo in December, 1931. Exiled under General Martínez, he returned after Martinéz's ouster only to die, still young, in 1947.

José Luis Barrientos also took no part in the events of 1932, but was a significant figure in the history of Salvadorean radicalism. He had been a student of law at the University of El Salvador at the same time as Recinos. During the regime of Carranza in Mexico, a number of radical Mexican students came to the university to spread the ideas of the Mexican Revolution. These ideas captured the minds of such men as

12. Ibid., pp. 48-50.
13. [Arias Gómez], *Martí*, pp. 15-16. Joaquín Castro Canizales remembers working with Recinos on the staff of *Diario Latino*.

Recinos, Barrientos, and Farabundo Martí. Barrientos was an energetic, tempestuous young man, capable of passionate loyalties and hatreds. His energy soon made him the recognized leader of the student radicals and something of a hero among the Salvadorean people. He founded a periodical, *La Ráfaga,* and through it waged bitter war against the dictatorial regimes of the brothers Meléndez. A poet as well as a journalist, he was capable of impassioned verses which became as celebrated as his more prosaic attacks on the government.

In February, 1920, when Jorge Meléndez was in power, a delegation of Guatemalan student exiles arrived in San Salvador with the intention of making propaganda against the dictatorship in Guatemala of the incredible tyrant Manuel Estrada Cabrera. Barrientos marked their arrival at the University of El Salvador by organizing a mass meeting in the capital's Parque Bolívar. As a result, the police moved in and arrested Barrientos and a number of his followers and friends. A few days later Jorge Meléndez ordered the young men marched from their cells into his presence. The name of Barrientos was especially well known to him as the author of a recently printed attack upon his brother Carlos, who had just died in a United States hospital. Among the other youths arrested were some from the first families of El Salvador: Salvador Escalón, Alonzo Argueta, and Ramón Giralt, among others. Therefore, the dictator planned to let them all off with a stern warning, except for the stiff-necked Barrientos. After a harangue, Meléndez announced his intention to free the rest but to confine the ring leader on a prison island in the Gulf of Fonseca.

One of the students, an unprepossessing dark-complexioned little student, heretofore unnoticed, spoke up, declaring that if all of them were guilty of the same offense (that is, being at the rally), then all of them ought to receive the same punishment. Of course, he knew the real reason for the exemplary punishment. The president flew into a rage. Made to look ridiculous, he did not carry out his original harsh intention, but instead he ordered that all might go free except Barrientos and this troublemaker. They were to be sent into exile.[14]

The audacious student was Agustín Farabundo Martí. Among the radical students he had the reputation of being the exact opposite of Barrientos. He was of a cool, calculating temperament, a sober and energetic worker. In appearance he was unexceptional, except for his very dark skin, and in his later pictures, especially the one taken just before his execution, Martí appears as a thin, sad-eyed man with a drooping mustache, the sort of man who might have been a bank teller or a shop assistant. But those who knew him had quite a different impression of "El Negro," as he was nicknamed for his complexion. Serefín Quiteño remembers him as a "reserved mestizo of strong, noble features with a broad forehead and tranquil, dark eyes." Although Quiteño goes on to add that Martí's basic character was that of a romantic intellectual with a "martyr complex," most of those who knew him remember better his intensity, passion, and logic in private discourse and the remarkable fact that when called upon to speak in public he was utterly incapable of doing so.[15] His vast erudition was also remarked on. He had read not only Marx and Lenin but most of the philosophers of the nineteenth century and the utopian socialists.

Martí was born in Teotepeque, a small town situated in a remote region of the department of La Libertad. He was the sixth of fourteen children born to the landholder Pedro Martí and Doña Socorro Rodríguez de Martí, who had married Don Pedro when she was only fourteen. Five of her children died in infancy, but nine survived which meant, later on, that the estate would have to be divided into numerous parcels.

The estate was not an inconsiderable one. Pedro Martí came from a family which had been poor *campesinos* but which had managed to rise to the local aristocracy. Pedro's estate consisted of two haciendas and a total of 1,280 hectares or about five

14. Ibid., pp. 1-2.
15. David Alejandro Luna, "Algunas facetas sociales en la vida de Agustín Farabundo Martí," *Revista Salvadoreña de Ciencias Sociales* 1 (January-March 1965): 100.

square miles of land. The marriage of Don Pedro and Doña Socorro (whose name seems somehow prophetic) was not a happy one. According to Dr. David Luna, they quarreled because of her jealous behavior, "for which there was ample cause." Eventually, Doña Socorro was put out to pasture with a small estate and two hundred head of cattle.[16]

Agustín Farabundo Martí was educated at the academy of the Salesian Fathers in the capital where he is said to have been not only a good student but a sports star. He received his *bachillerato* (the equivalent of a North American high school diploma) in 1913 or 1914. He entered the National University in 1914, but immediately began to get into trouble. In those days the dominant philosophy was the positivism of Comte, and Martí, whose tastes ran to Hegel and Marx, found himself in violent conflict with his professor of philosophy, Dr. Victorino López Ayala. After several classroom battles in which at least once they descended to personal abuse, Martí challenged his teacher to a duel. This battle was fortunately avoided through the intercession of friends, but it illustrated how seriously the young student took his convictions and how little ready he was to compromise or accept the give and take of university life. Martí was well on his way to becoming the fanatic whose drive and determination were to make him the terror of his enemies.[17]

More happy when discussing Marx or playing politics than when working seriously on his law degree, Martí never completed his studies, although, between exiles, he attended classes through the twenties. It is quite possible that he welcomed the incident which exiled him from the country in February, 1920, when he spoke out on behalf of Barrientos before the president.

Exile, despite its economic hardships, was in many ways the best thing that could happen to a young Salvadorean leftist in those days. Exile meant the opportunity to travel and learn new ideas, to meet new comrades, and to rethink one's own positions.

16. Ibid., pp. 90-91; [Arias Gómez], *Martí*, pp. 2-3; de la Selva, "Lucha," p. 197. The last source says Martí was born in 1894, but Luna and Arias Gómez give 1893 as his birth date.
17. [Arias Gómez], *Martí*, pp. 3-4; Luna, "Vida de Martí," pp. 91-95.

Barrientos, the student leader, went to Guatemala, and there his views soon earned him the title of "the Bolshevik" among the students at that university. While there he received word that his family was being dispossessed from their estate by the government, in a move of quasi-legal revenge. Perhaps this strengthened Barrientos's determination to master the law. He studied at Tegucigalpa and there obtained the right to practice. As a lawyer, Barrientos was active in Central America, and at last returned to El Salvador where he fought to restore the rights of his family.[18] Concern with the law appears to have made him more conservative and he drifted out of radical circles.

His friend Martí, on the other hand, was in the process of becoming more radical. He looked like a mild-mannered man, but he thought deeply, and unlike most of the radical students, he was capable of putting his thoughts into decisive actions when the chance came. Men did not notice him at first, but when he spoke, they listened. According to later legend, Martí went to Mexico and participated in the closing struggles of the Mexican Revolution as a member of the "Red Guards," but chronologically, as Mauricio de la Selva points out, this is impossible.[19] It appears that he went first into Honduras and then crossed into Guatemala. There he lived for some time in the capital, with a sister who came from El Salvador to take care of him. From time to time he disappeared from the view of his sister and his radical student friends at the university. During these mysterious disappearances he is said to have worked at various menial tasks—as a distiller for the "El Zapote" firm, as a construction laborer, as a *campesino*. He was trying to learn firsthand the nature of the regime he was fighting. From exile, Martí bitterly denounced the formation of the Liga Roja as a petit bourgeois attempt to sidetrack the working class.

18. Jorge Schlesinger, *Revolución comunista*, pp. 34-36.
19. De la Selva, "Lucha," pp. 200-201; Luna, in "Vida de Martí," pp. 96-97, accepts this story as true. It is possible, but unlikely, that he had joined briefly in the revolt of Adolpho de la Huerta in 1923.

In 1925 the Partido Socialista Centroamericano was formed in Guatemala City. Martí and two Salvadorean friends, Miguel Angel Vásquez, an older radical, and Moisés Castro y Morales, were among the charter members. This organization was really the beginning of communist activity in Central America. That same year the president of Guatemala, José María Orellana, decided that foreign leftists must go. Martí and Miguel Angel Vásquez were forced to leave. They went to San Salvador and took up residence in a house in the city. Here Martí began his association with the Federación Regional de Trabajadores de El Salvador. He worked furiously for the organization, punching away at his typewriter like a man possessed, turning out reams of propaganda and memoranda. When Quiñónez Molina heard of his presence in the capital he exiled him again, but Martí soon slipped back into the country and resumed his activities.[20]

Very soon Martí established himself among intellectual circles in San Salvador. The principal gathering place for young intellectuals in those days was a cafe on the east side of the square in front of the Teatro Nacional. Here Martí got to know many of the rising literary men of the country. He became a member of the literary circle around Joaquín Castro Canizales, Quino Caso, as he always signs himself. Many of those he associated with did not know the true identity of the man referred to simply as El Negro.

In those days Martí wore a red star on his lapel with a picture of Leon Trotsky on it. At this time, of course, Trotsky was in disgrace, but not yet anathema. It would be fair to say, however, that Martí was much more like Trotsky in character than like Stalin. During 1930 and 1931 Martí did, of course, accept whatever aid he could get from the dictator of Russia (which was very little), but it would be wrong to think of this temperamental and passionate Salvadorean as a Stalinist. As his biographer, Jorge Arias Gómez, put it to me, Martí was "loosely associated with the Third International."

When Pío Romero Bosque became president of El Salvador in 1927 the university students took advantage of the new breath

20. Luna, "Vida de Martí," pp. 98-99; de la Selva, "Lucha," p. 202; [Arias Gómez], *Martí*, pp. 7-8.

of freedom to form a student organization known as *Asociación General de Estudiantes Universitarios Salvadoreños*, or AGEUS, a group which continues in existence to this day. These students were generally dissatisfied with Salvadorean politics, but few were genuine leftists, and very few Marxists. However, in the late twenties many university students went out into the countryside as part of the radical education program of the FRTS known as the "popular university." A clandestine Communist Youth International group also formed.[21]

In 1927 Martí began to be persecuted by the government; Don Pío always walked the narrow line between permissiveness and repression. Imprisoned, Martí went on a hunger strike and the university students organized themselves to come to his aid. Pedro Geoffroy Rivas believes that student pressure, combined with his hunger strike, succeeded in freeing him. If so, it offered a foretaste of the tactics which Martí was to use so successfully in 1931. The students of AGEUS, although not Marxist in orientation, began to look up to him as a popular hero for the simple reason that he appeared as the uncompromising enemy of all bourgeois authority.

By 1928 Martí was finding life in El Salvador difficult because of government persecution, and he felt the need for strengthening his contacts abroad. Personally, there was little in El Salvador to hold him. He had given away his lands in Teotepeque, and there was little chance of his finishing his law studies and pursuing a career in El Salvador. The spring of 1928 found him in New York City at the headquarters of the Anti-Imperialist League, where he was on one occasion picked up in a police raid.[22] It was perhaps at this time that he became a leader in the SRI movement which he later headed in El Salvador. In the month of May he decided to go back to Central America, this time to Nicaragua, where General Augusto Sandino was beginning his anti-Yankee campaign.

---

21. Marroquín, "Crisis," p. 46; National Archives, Record Group 59, Sussdorff from Latvia, October 5, 1928, file 816.00B/8. This collection is hereafter referred to as N.A., R.G. 59, plus file number.
22. Luna, "Vida de Martí," p. 99.

Sandino was the illegitimate son of a small landholder. When the liberals resisted American intervention, Sandino had joined them enthusiastically. But by 1928, most of the liberal generals had laid down their arms in return for Yankee promises. Not so Sandino, who organized a pitiful guerrilla remnant and continued to fight. Despite heavy losses he held off the U.S. Marines for some time.

Martí went first to Mexico from New York, then to Cuba, and from there to Jamaica. He entered Guatemala from Belice under the guise of a *chiclero* (a chicle harvester). From there he slipped into Tegucigalpa, Honduras, where he met with Sandino's agents, who accepted his credentials as a revolutionary and packed him off into the back country toward the Nicaraguan border. About the same time that Martí reached Sandino's camp, Esteban Pavletich also arrived and the two became good friends and close associates of Sandino.

In a letter to a friend, Martí wrote, "We arrived at the encampment of our supreme chief, General Augusto César Sandino, on the 22nd of June, desiring to join the army of sovereign national defense. Our war against the invaders of Central America is now formally launched. In Nicaragua the liberating struggle of the Americas has begun and it is to be hoped that the joint action of all the oppressed lands of the continent will sweep away the last vestiges of Yankee imperialism."[23]

Although Sandino and his associates did all that they could, the great anti-Yankee revolt never came. New elections in Nicaragua in November, 1928, resulted in a more stable and popular government. The Marines gradually turned more of the military duties over to local *guardia*. By July, 1929, Sandino was forced to ask for a safe conduct to Mexico for himself and his followers. Martí accompanied him to Mérida, Mexico, as his personal secretary.

During the year that he was with the Sandino movement, Martí never ceased trying to convert his leader to communism. But Sandino was not the sort of man to interest himself in

23. Pineda, "Tragedia comunista," *Diario de Hoy*, February 7, 1967. This letter is dated September 26, 1928.

dialectic, and besides, his attitudes remained those of a small landholder. He was a national patriotic leader, and Martí's socialist preachings were a source of embarrassment to the movement, which actually had to defend itself against charges of being socialistic in order to win support at home and abroad. The two men were still on good terms when their party passed through El Salvador on the way to Mexico in June, 1929. Luis Felipe Recinos, who was at this time cooking up the idea of "popular universities" to educate the masses to radicalism, wrote a glowing tribute to both men.[24]

According to one story, the break between Martí and Sandino came in Mérida when Martí tried to convince Sandino that the Mexican government was trying to poison him. Sandino, presumably annoyed by this almost pathological suggestion, then dismissed Martí. More likely, the break occurred when Martí at last gave up on his attempts to convince Sandino of the virtues of international Marxism. At any rate, the actual parting was smoothed over by the pretense that Martí was being sent on a special mission to Mexico City, in August, 1929. Martí gave "ill health" as his reason for not rejoining the movement at a later date. Sandino on his part is said to have lamented Martí's loss "as much as the loss of a battle," which might not be too much, considering the number of battles Sandino had lost. In December a rumor filtered back to El Salvador that Martí had become mentally disturbed in Yucatán and was in a mental hospital. It is possible that he suffered a mental collapse at the time of his break with Sandino, and this may shed some light on the "poisoning" episode; but Martí, although high-strung, was anything but a madman, and any derangement was temporary.[25]

In a February, 1931, letter to his friend the Uruguayan poet Blanca Luz Brum, Martí said: "My break with Sandino was not, as is sometimes said, for divergence of moral principles or opposing norms of conduct....He would not embrace my communist program. His banner was only that of national

24. N.A., R.G. 59, Report of General Conditions in El Salvador, June 29, 1929, file 816.00B.
25. De la Selva, "Lucha," p. 200. The rumor of poisoning is from N.A., R.G. 59, General Conditions in El Salvador, December 5, 1929, file 816.00/716.

independence,...not social revolution....I solemnly declare that General Sandino is the greatest patriot in the world."[26]

After leaving the Sandino forces, Martí did, in fact, go to Mexico City. His mother, completely estranged now from his father (who, it is interesting to note, was at this time *alcalde* of Teotepeque) was living there, either in order to be closer to her son, or for reasons of health. In the period from November, 1929, to February, 1930, he lived with Doña Socorro, who was ill. At one time he was arrested and briefly jailed by the Mexican government for allegedly taking part in the abortive coup of Daniel Flores against the authorities. The spring of 1930 found Martí in Guatemala City where he received a briefing on conditions in El Salvador from Miguel Angel Vásquez and Jorge Fernandéz Anaya.[27] The exact date of his return to El Salvador is not known, because he entered the country quietly, but it was certainly between May 1 and June 1 of 1930. Once back in El Salvador he lost no time in taking advantage of the last chaotic days of the Pío Romero Bosque administration.

In the end, it was to be Martí who would lead the doomed forces of the proletariat to the uprising of January, 1932. Of the other men mentioned above, only Miguel Mármol played a significant part in the Salvadorean revolt, along with Martí's other lieutenants, Ismael Hernández and Rafael Bondanza. Like the countless revolutionaries who had paved the way for Lenin, most of the earlier leaders in the revolutionary struggle had passed from the immediate scene of action before their efforts could bear fruit.

26. De La Selva, "Lucha," p. 202.
27. Ibid., p. 205.

Chapter 3
The Election of Arturo Araujo

Don Pío Romero Bosque, the president since March, 1927, was doing his best to head off the discontent fostered by Fernández Anaya and Martí. Since his election he had talked much of the "scientific organization of labor," and had passed laws regulating the hours of work in some industries in July, 1928, and April, 1929. Further, a law regulating compensation in work accidents had been put into effect shortly after he took office.[1]

Romero Bosque was, in fact, quite ready to play along with unionism as long as it did not directly affect the chief supporters of his government, the coffee growers. When, however, he discovered that by the middle of 1930 the newly Marxist FRTS had organized some eighty thousand agricultural workers, he became distinctly alarmed. On August 12, 1930, a decree came from the government prohibiting agitation and workers' rallies, as well as the printing or circulating of Marxist propaganda. The post office was empowered to confiscate such subversive literature. This was all aimed at prohibiting a recurrence of the great petition of April, and Fernández Anaya's May Day parade. The August decree did not work. Instead the FRTS redoubled its activities among agricultural workers, while the Marxist organizations only throve under persecution.

The government was forced to back its words with deeds. A "white terror" reigned during August and September, 1930. The *guardia* and the National Police rounded up no less than six hundred *campesinos* in Sonsonate department for signing a manifesto of protest against the August 12 decree. Others were taken around Santa Tecla for trying to organize a chapter of

1. Jacinto Paredes, *Vida y obras del Dr. Pío Romero Bosque: Apuntes para la historia de El Salvador* (San Salvador, 1930), pp. 337-38.

SRI. All these agitators received fines and many were given jail sentences. Nothing, of course, could have pleased SRI and the Communist party more. A "Campaign for the Liberation of Political Prisoners" was organized. This was met with fresh repression. A decree on October 30 forbade all demonstrations of peasants' or workers' organizations against stores, individuals, or the authorities—a sure sign that the August decree had not worked. On November 27 there was a violent clash in Santa Ana where a street demonstration had to be smashed by the police.

In that same month, Don Pío tried to ease tensions somewhat by freeing most of those taken in August and September; but four days before Christmas, General Leitzeler, the commander of the police, committed an exemplary massacre in Santa Ana, killing the organizer, Pedro Alonzo, and seven of his followers. Between the middle of November and the end of February, 1931, when Pío Romero Bosque left office, about twelve hundred persons were imprisoned for left-wing activities or labor agitation.[2] One of the victims of these measures was the communist chief Agustín Farabundo Martí, who was thus out of the way during the election of 1931.

Perhaps it was partly to regain the general popularity that had attended the beginning of his presidency that Don Pío made his fateful decision to open the electoral campaign for the presidency to all comers. At any rate, the decision had been made by the spring of 1930 and the newspapers of the capital soon bulged with rumors concerning the campaign.

Unfortunately, since such an election had never been held before, there was absolutely no machinery of democracy in operation. There was no two-party system; indeed, there was no real party system at all, but simply a number of caudillos, local chieftains supported by their own followers. There were no party primaries, no screening of candidates. The result was a reasonably free, but very chaotic, election.

By May 11, 1930, there were three candidates, Dr. Miguel Tomás Molina, Dr. Enrique Córdova, and Dr. Alberto Gómez

2. [Arias Gómez], Martí, p. 180; de la Selva, "Lucha," p. 198; Italo López Vallecillos, El periodismo en El Salvador: Basquejo histórico-documental... (San Salvador, 1964), pp. 158-59.

Zárate. This last named was the man the president was thought to favor, and under normal circumstances he would have been the surefire winner with a generous 75 percent of the recorded vote. However, when it became clear that Pío Romero Bosque was indeed serious about holding a free election, there was a mad scramble to get on the list of candidates. General Maximiliano Hernández Martínez, a well-known military man and theosophist, resigned his position as second inspector general of the army on May 28 and threw his hat in the ring. A more prominent general, Antonio Claramount Lucero, did likewise.

The candidates were as confused as anyone else as to how the election campaign was to be conducted. Accordingly, they held a meeting on June 13 to work out the rules for the forthcoming election, and possibly, to decide the winner in advance. Only Dr. Córdova refused to take part. As it turned out, however, none of these distinguished gentlemen was to gain the honor of the presidency. On the contrary, the prize was destined to go to the candidate of the "masses."

The fact was that the growing labor movement in El Salvador did not find any of these candidates to its liking. This is not surprising, for all the candidates represented some facet of conservative interests. Gómez Zárate's group represented a continuation of the highly bureaucratic and centralized policies of Quiñónez Molina. On the other hand, the Constitutionalist party headed by Molina had been formed in opposition to Quiñónez Molina and was considered to be the party of the progressive middle-class elements. The National Evolutionary party of Enrique Córdova was largely a group of irate landholders with more or less progressive tendencies. General Claramount Lucero was an extreme conservative, while General Hernández Martínez, who tried to woo labor with a series of almost socialist articles, was an unknown quantity at that point.[3]

As a result, the labor movement began to search for someone who exemplified the ideals of the masses—not a poor man, to be sure, but someone from the ruling aristocracy who would be willing to announce himself as the champion of the

3. Wilson, "Crisis of National Integration," p. 201.

poor. So it was that various labor groups, especially in the densely settled western part of the country, seized upon the name of Don Arturo Araujo. Don Arturo had formerly been a supporter of Dr. Córdova. He was first mentioned as a possible candidate in *Diario del Salvador* on May 20, 1930, but it was not until July 4 that he officially decided that he would become the champion of labor.[4]

Don Arturo Araujo was a well-built man with a high forehead, ruddy cheeks, deep-set, penetrating eyes, and an aquiline nose. He looked not unlike the novelist Vladimir Nabokov, except that he generally wore a beatific smile. Araujo was, as a former supporter described him, "a good, generous man," whose "purse was always open."[5] The latter quality helped to make him an ideal candidate. However, Araujo is a man much maligned in Salvadorean history. The typical version is presented in Francisco Machón Vilanova's novel *Ola Roja*, a book about the 1932 revolt which is of dubious literary merit but considerable historical interest. In the novel Don Arturo is described as being "as bland of heart as he was inept in politics."[6] There is almost, but not quite, universal agreement on this characterization.

At the time, however, Araujo seemed the ideal man to lead the country which was, as the campaign started, already beginning to feel the effects of the Great Depression. The candidate had been born in Suchitoto in 1878, the son of a wealthy landholding family. Throughout his youth he had known considerable luxury and his family was able to send him abroad to complete his education. He chose to take up the field of engineering, an unusual choice for his time and social standing. He studied this subject at the University of London, and went on from there to study languages in Zurich. He became an accomplished linguist, able to speak fluently in English, German, French, and Italian. Back in England once more, he decided to gain practical experience in the British factory

4. Jorge Schlesinger, *Revolución comunista*, p. 20.
5. "Recollections of 'XX,'" in Pineda, "Tragedia comunista," *Diario de Hoy*, January 18, 1967.
6. Francisco Machón Vilanova, *Ola roja* (Mexico, 1948), p. 334.

system. He moved to Liverpool and applied his engineering talents to industry. Meanwhile, he boarded at the house of a shop steward who was also an important official of the Labour party. This was hardly the prescribed course for an aristocrat from El Salvador. He added to his cosmopolitanism by marrying Dora Morton, an English girl of good family, who returned with him to El Salvador in 1900.

At home, he became the "good landlord," paying double the going rate to his employees, and doing much to beautify the provincial town of Armenia in western El Salvador, where he spent a good deal of his time.[7] He also became a leader of popular discontent against the dictatorial ways of the Meléndez family. In 1922 he backed a revolt which began in the northern town of Arcatao. The movement failed because of a lack of local support,[8] but it helped Araujo by establishing his liberal credentials. From all this it might be presumed that he was anything but bland and, as we shall see, the problems of his presidency arose more from the pressure of events than from the personality of the president. At the time he announced his candidacy he was widely hailed as a decisive and able man. On the other hand, the shrewd North American charge, W. W. Schott, wrote to Washington that Araujo "is a splendid gentleman who has done much for the progress of his country," but he added, "his friends, however, concur in the opinion that he had best leave politics alone."[9]

Meanwhile, as the campaign progressed, Salvadoreans began to fall into the spirit of the thing and work earnestly for their candidates. Pío Romero Bosque basked in extravagant praise for the simple fact that he had allowed the public to choose his successor. One paper declared that he had "broken forever with the traditions of the past," and called him "El Salvador's greatest president."[10]

7. Luna, "Trágico suceso," p. 57; Mercedes Durand, "Entrevista con el expresidente Don Arturo Araujo," *Diario Latino*, January 5, 1968.
8. Wilson, *National Integration*, p. 163.
9. N.A., R.G. 59, W.W. Schott to Secretary of State, February 3, 1930, file 816.00/766.
10. *Diario del Salvador*, September 1, 1930; see also Paredes, p. 250.

But it may well have been that El Salvador's greatest president soon began to have second thoughts about the wisdom of his course. The truth was that he would probably have favored Gómez Zárate had not that candidate been so identified with the policies of Jorge Meléndez. Since Don Pío was supposed to represent a reform tendency, this made backing him impossible, and the president was unable to choose between Córdova and Molina, the reformist candidates. From this dilemma came his decision to throw the election open to all comers. One thing was certain: to the ruling elite, Arturo Araujo, a renegade and nonconformist, was only marginally acceptable at best.

Don Arturo's supporters began to form what they called the Labor party, modeled after the British Labour party which Araujo so admired. It was not a preexisting organization which drafted Araujo as its candidate, but rather a kind of ad hoc party made up on the spur of the moment to take advantage of the unheard-of windfall of free elections. In its spontaneity it was typical of El Salvador's political parties both before that time and since. These labor party men, many of them representing noncommunist splinters of the FRTS, engaged in a vigorous campaign, stressing the "class struggle" element and getting an ill-deserved reputation as wild-eyed Marxist radicals. Luis Felipe Recinos, an ex-communist journalist and labor leader who had started the "popular universities" to educate the masses, and the noted labor theorist Professor Miguel Angel Martínez, along with a clique of university students, made every effort to stress that Araujo's aims were revolutionary which, in fact, they were not. Eventually Araujo had to break with Recinos, at least publicly. The latter then formed his own party, the Partido Proletariado Salvadoreño. This splinter group continued to campaign for Araujo, probably doing him more harm than good.

Arturo Araujo was understandably displeased at the kind of image he was getting. He was smart enough to know that he had to attract not only the urban mechanics or the peasants, who probably would not vote in any numbers, but also a large segment of the enlightened middle and lower middle classes.

Thus desirous of evading a Marxist taint, he turned to *vitalismo,* a doctrine concocted by the celebrated local savant, Don Alberto Masferrer, who is greatly admired to this day as the greatest prose writer in the history of El Salvador.

Masferrer was, as Alejandro D. Marroquín has put it, "a typical Salvadoreño, a mestizo,...and an illegitimate child."[11] He was a man of great education and culture who had traveled extensively in South America and Europe. In the twenties he had founded the newspaper *Patria,* which, though short lived, was a great contribution to the journalism of the country. Often styled a communist by his political foes, he was in reality hardly even a socialist. Some have called him an "anarcho-socialist," but the truth is that his doctrines, in so far as one can make them out, were those of a reformer advocating free enterprise and the welfare state.[12] Evidently Masferrer looked upon himself as a disciple of Henry George, but he did not follow George's ideas with any consistency. *Vitalismo* referred to the "vital minimum" which Masferrer declared that all should have in order to live a decent human life. He included nine major points, among them: hygienic, honest work; sufficient, varied, and nutritious food; good housing; medical and sanitary care; expedient and honest justice; decent education; and rest and recreation. He was also a noted temperance advocate, as was Araujo, and wanted to bring an end to the time-honored Salvadoreño custom of the lower classes drinking themselves into a machete-wielding fury every weekend.

To achieve his goals, Masferrer declared, the state should set aside other matters such as useless military expenditure and sink its wealth into the betterment of the social conditions of all.[13] This was a sensible and appealing idea, though its author left not a clue as to how it was to be effectively carried out. Even more appealing to the people of El Salvador was his idea of land reform. Already at that time many people were being forced to migrate into Honduras to find land, while the size of

11. Marroquín, "Crisis," p. 43.
12. Graciela Bográn, in *En torno a Masferrer,* by Ministerio de Educación (San Salvador, 1956), p. 231. This is a collection of essays by Bográn, Pedro Geoffroy Rivas, Quino Caso, and others.
13. Alberto Masferrer, *Minimun vital* (San Salvador, n.d.), pp.15, 25.

estates in El Salvador seemed to be growing. "Disgracefully," he declared, "the land is not as free as the air, and men are able to monopolize it." To prevent this he recommended a redistribution of the soil hoping, in some indefinite way, to create a race of yeoman farmers.[14] The chief difference between Marx and Masferrer was that the latter did not believe in the class struggle as a means of achieving his aims. He hoped, optimistically, that the rich could be persuaded to tax themselves enough so that the government could buy up part of the land and give it to the poor. Arturo Araujo, a much more level-headed and practical man, probably had no intention of trying most of the scholar's theories.

During the election campaign, Don Alberto Masferrer campaigned vigorously for the Labor party cause. "The country has had for its governor citizens of every sort," he declared in a campaign speech. "It has had in the presidency lawyers, farmers, soldiers, doctors, but not until now a man of such generosity and heart. And for this reason I am with Arturo Araujo, for this reason I have followed him. Because such a man can resolve the problems of the country and give to all a better life."[15] But the masses of the people could not have read Masferrer's books, and had little idea of the theories of Henry George. They gained only the hazy idea that somehow Masferrer and Araujo would get them all out of the economic crisis that was gripping the country. The election campaign filled the common folk with restlessness and a vague ambition which would mean trouble for a Labor party regime unless it was able quickly to fulfill its promises of a better life for the people.

The support of Masferrer and Recinos, both of whom appeared redder than Trotsky to the excitable elite, lessened the chances that the ruling classes and the military would allow Araujo to win in a free election. Up through the first week of January most observers believed Romero Bosque's promise of absolute electoral honesty, but then rumors began to come out that if Araujo was the popular winner, there might be trouble.

14. Alberto Masferrer, *Cartas a un obrero* (San Salvador, n.d.) pp. 17-18.
15. Pineda, 'Tragedia comunista," *Diario de Hoy*, January 18, 1967.

On the first day of the balloting in the three-day election, Araujo ran up a commanding lead, partly due to the fact that General Maximiliano Hernández Martínez, an army officer suddenly infected with reforming zeal, had mysteriously dropped from the race at the last moment and given his backing to the Labor party candidate. Araujo's success prompted Warren D. Robbins, the United States minister to El Salvador, to cable Washington asking that a "battleship" be held ready in case of trouble. In response, the U.S.S. *Sacramento* was dispatched to Corinto, Nicaragua, and held there until after the new president was inaugurated.[16]

Don Pío made no effort to influence the electoral decision, but as the balloting progressed General Claramount charged fraud at the polls and on the thirteenth began to sound out officers about a coup. General Enrique Leitzeler, the chief of police, then dispatched his men to strategic positions around San Salvador and blocked Claramount's intentions. In the end, as Robbins remarked, the election "was carried through in admirable fashion."[17]

When all the votes were counted, Arturo Araujo had 101,069 votes, with 62,931 cast for Gómez Zárate, 32,778 for Enrique Cordóva, 16,464 for the disgruntled General Claramount, and 4,163 for Molina, according to the tabulation of *Diario Latino* on January 15, 1931. Despite the fact that Araujo had collected more votes than the next two candidates combined, he did not have the simple majority of all votes cast which the constitution required for election. Thus on January 20 the election was declared thrown into the unicameral legislature. In theory, the assembly could vote for any of the three highest candidates, but in fact there was little danger that they would not abide by the will of the people and put into office the overwhelming popular choice. This was especially true because after the balloting Dr. Córdova gave Araujo his support, and between the two they had an easy majority of supporters in the newly elected legislature. In later years,

16. N.A., R.G. 59, file 816.00/786.
17. N.A., R.G. 59, Robbins to Secretary of State, January 14, 1931, file 816.00/787.

Araujo himself mentioned with pride "the atmosphere of democracy and absolute freedom" which surrounded his election.[18] On February 12, 1931, he was declared the unanimous winner.

But between the popular election and the balloting by the legislature, new developments came to light. Warren D. Robbins, who had great respect for Don Arturo, wrote his government on January 23 that his only worry over Araujo's election was the financial situation of the victorious candidate. "He was a very rich land owner until a year ago," the minister explained, "but owing to his political activity for the last year he has neglected his coffee business and has mortgaged his properties in the country and in town to the extent of more than two million colones." With these debts, plus those which the outgoing president had given the country, the diplomat speculated that Araujo, who was, he said, "a very honest man," might have a hard time. The report of the U.S. military attache in Costa Rica, who received information from former dictator Jorge Meléndez, was even grimmer. Lt. Col. Fred T. Cruse put Araujo's debts at $1,700,000 and added that his creditors would have bankrupted him had he not been a candidate. With less faith in human nature than Robbins, Cruse suggested, unfairly, that Araujo would recoup his loss at public expense. The latter report appears to have exaggerated the debts, due no doubt to Melendez's dislike of Araujo. In a later dispatch Cruse himself estimated Araujo's debt to be 400,000 colones.[19]

Whatever the exact state of the new president's personal finances, he was starting his rule in a period of trouble and great hope. His reign, begun in democracy, was destined to last only nine months before it was overthrown in blood and violence, and its overthrow would lead, two months later, to the much bloodier events of January, 1932.

18. Durand, "Entrevista," *Diario Latino*, January 5, 1968.
19. N.A., R.G., 59, Robbins to Secretary of State, January 23, 1931, file 816.00/793; Ibid., Lt. Col. Fred T. Cruse to Secretary of State, file 816.00/798 and /800.

Chapter 4

Araujo's Presidency and the Coup of December 2

In the elections of January, 1931, the people had overwhelmingly chosen Don Arturo Araujo. Their choice had been duly ratified by the legislature when it unanimously chose him president. Despite the problems of the depression it was expected that his regime would accomplish great things. He represented a new dawning of democracy in a coup-ridden country, scientific expertise in a land where lawyers and colonels generally ruled. He was a cosmopolitan in a nation noted for its provincialism. Certainly, no foreign government welcomed him more warmly than that of the United States. U.S. minister Warren D. Robbins hastened to pay his respects to the president-elect as soon as the choice was official.

Yet, within weeks of taking over on March 1, the government was in serious trouble. Dissatisfaction showed in every social class, and within nine months the government was toppled. To explain these events, a legend has grown up in El Salvador concerning the regime of Arturo Araujo. According to this legend, Don Arturo, who everyone agrees was a good, generous, and sincere man, found himself surrounded by hordes of office seekers. To these men he said generously, "Take over the offices and select what you want," but unfortunately there were not enough to go around. Even when men of long experience were sacked, the rapacious *laboristas* could not be satisfied. They were enjoying power for the first time in history, and lording it over the aristocratic classes who had been at least briefly defeated. When they saw that the spoils were not enough, they began to grow restive. The popularity of good Don Arturo went downhill from the moment he took the presidential oath.[1]

This legend simplifies what was in reality a very complex situation. Araujo had to placate many conflicting interests: landlords, workers, peasants, the military, his own party. He had to meet that challenge in the face of a world-wide depression and of growing pressure from Martí and the extreme left. The most important element to be satisfied was the military, who must have watched the freedom of the elections with some misgivings. It was evident to Arturo Araujo that they would have to be convinced to give their support to the regime. One minor element in the victory of the labor candidate had been the last-minute endorsement by General Maximiliano Hernández Martínez (who is always referred to in Salvadorean history as General Martínez, rather than General Hernández). While it is doubtful that General Martínez influenced many voters, he was one military man who seemed to be favorable to the new regime. Although it is probable that Araujo was truthful in asserting later that he had made no bargain with the general ahead of time, Martínez was not slow in presenting his bill after the election. A Masonic brother of the general approached the president-elect and suggested that since, according to Salvadorean custom, he must select a vice-president, General Martínez would be the ideal man for the job.

Araujo evidently welcomed this suggestion. Martínez was not the leading officer in the army, but he was widely respected. He had never expressed his political views to any extent, but his support seemed to indicate that he would favor Labor party policies. Only one condition did the president-elect make, that the general marry his long-time mistress, Concha Monteagudo, by whom he had several children. Araujo, still envisioning the British Parliament as his model, thought it unseemly that the vice-president of El Salvador should be living

---

1. Pineda, in "Tragedia comunista," *Diario de Hoy*, January 17 and 18, 1967, presents a perfect example of this legend.

in sin. Martínez agreed to the stipulation and Don Arturo was their best man.[2]

What is more difficult to explain is why the new president was so naive as to entrust the same man not only with the vice-presidency but also with the ministry of war. In a way the choice was logical, as Martínez was an experienced officer, but politically it was an open invitation for a coup d'etat. The truth seems to be that Araujo had an exaggerated trust in the general, in spite of rather bizarre personal characteristics on the part of the latter. As time went on, Martínez became increasingly preoccupied with exotic and occult religious manifestations, and even when he assumed the vice-presidency he was a convinced theosophist and believed in the transmigration of human souls into other persons.[3] During his years as president of El Salvador he achieved a reputation as a witch doctor, and was popularly nicknamed El Brujo. He sold home remedies to his constituents as a cure for everything from toothache to earthquake. Seances were said to be common at his home.

The army that the new minister inherited appears to have been a good one. Pío Romero Bosque, who had been minister of war under his predecessor, had worked for eight years on military reforms. On coming to power the Labor party found that a high standard of training and efficiency already existed in the three-thousand-man force.[4] Nevertheless, the new minister found it necessary to conduct a wholesale purge of the leading officers and to put in men who were loyal to the new government and especially to himself.[5] Going beyond this, General Martínez soon began the formation of a Directorio Militar composed of the higher officers, to manipulate the government from behind the scenes. It was not an uncommon

2. Durand, "Entrevista," *Diario Latino*, January 5, 1968. This is Arturo Araujo's own version in his last interview.
3. John D. Martz, *Central America: The Crisis and the Challenge* (Chapel Hill, N.C.: University of North Carolina Press, 1959), p. 82.
4. Gen. Salvador Peña Trejo, "Narración histórica de la insurrección militar de 2 de diciembre de 1931," *Diario Latino*, April 24, 1964.
5. Col. Gregorio Bustamante Maceo, *Historia militar de El Salvador* (San Salvador, 1951), p. 105.

practice, a similar group having been formed behind the government of Don Pío Romero Bosque in 1927.[6]

The course of the new government did not run smoothly. Arturo Araujo took over the presidential palace, located in downtown San Salvador on what is now the site of the beautiful but almost empty National Library, on March 1. Two days later, on the third, he found himself besieged by thousands of peasants and laborers who had come to remind him of his government's promises to bring about reform. They shouted that they wanted land reform now.[7] The bewildered president appeared on his balcony and tried to calm the crowd; they only shouted all the louder. This went on for three days, and certainly must have made it difficult for the new government to get down to business. Another obstacle was the problem of selecting men to hold important offices in the Labor regime. The old oligarchy who thought Don Pío mad for holding free elections in the first place were horrified at the result of his folly. They refused to cooperate and to accept posts in the government. But whatever technical ability there was in El Salvador was concentrated in their hands. As a result, inexperienced Labor party men had to be brought in to fill important posts.[8]

Some oligarches were willing to play ball, for a price. According to Don Arturo himself, a group of bankers approached him and offered him a personal bribe of 500,000 colones if he would devalue the currency to 2.50 to the dollar. He refused on the grounds that devaluation would aid only the rich. The bankers withdrew in a huff.[9]

Not only was the government in trouble on the right before it even began to govern; it also found itself increasingly unable to satisfy with its programs those who had brought it to power.

6. Joaquín Castro Canizales [Quino Caso], "Narración histórica de la insurrección militar del 2 de diciembre de 1931: Acotaciones, aclaraciones y rectificaciones al estudio del General Salvador Peña Trejo," MS, 1:2. This copy is in the possession of Sr. Castro. A later version was published in *Diario Latino*, June, 1964.
7. Peña Trejo, "Narración histórico," *Diario Latino*, April 24, 1964.
8. Marroquín, "Crisis," p. 48.
9. Durand, "Entrevista," *Diario Latino*, January 5, 1968.

Araujo's program, as announced in *Patria* on March 1, 1931, consisted in: (1) limiting the sale of alcoholic beverages to six hours a day and lessening the dependence of the government on the rum tax (Araujo and Masferrer were temperance men); (2) using the army as a vast school for the primary education of the illiterate recruits; (3) increasing the water supply; (4) improving municipal administration by allowing locally collected taxes to be plowed back into local needs; (5) protecting Salvadorean labor from foreign competition (a measure aimed largely at resident Chinese); (6) reorganizing the school system and constructing more schools; (7) raising and protecting the status of women; (8) reforming the university; and (9) establishing a free medical aid program throughout the country. Only the last was even vaguely socialistic.

The same day the program came out, *Opinión Estudiantil* ran a blistering attack on the regime, which caused Araujo to briefly jail the student editor. More serious was the almost immediate defection of Alberto Masferrer. The U.S. attache in San Jose, Lt. Col. Fred T. Cruse, noted in a message to the State Department on March 23 that Masferrer "has become openly communistic, at least as far as his writings are concerned."[10] What this meant was that Masferrer, a member of the unicameral legislature, had begun to see that Labor party hacks were grabbing all the jobs. He himself had been offered a ministry and declined, expressing his distaste at the way the government leaders were feathering their nests and neglecting the poor. From the floor of the National Assembly he addressed the president, saying: "Don Arturo, listen to the voice of your friends and do not hear the voice of flatterers who surround you. Do not see as white that which some of us see as black. Don Arturo, don't get dragged into the mire, don't soil your reputation."[11]

Masferrer's attack deeply wounded the president, who continued to respect the philosopher. Years later, shortly before his death, Araujo remarked, "I cultivated a great friendship for

10. N.A., R.G. 59, file 816.00/800.
11. "Recollections of 'XX,'" in Pineda, "Tragedia comunista," *Diario de Hoy,* January 18, 1967.

Don Alberto Masferrer and retain great respect for his memory, and I believe that the knowledge which he had of the aspirations of our people played a large part in my victory. Don Alberto was not a communist, as many have said, but a great thinker with a tremendous human sensitivity."[12]

Even worse for the Labor party chief than the defection of his greatest intellectual supporter were persistent labor troubles, which, as we shall see, were assiduously cultivated by FRTS and the real communists. In April and May a series of important peasant strikes took place which were bloodily repressed by the army and *guardia* under the direction of General Martínez, the minister of war. "President Araujo is handling affairs in El Salvador much more firmly than had been expected," noted Cruse from Costa Rica, adding that the president was relying increasingly on Martínez.[13]

In July, faced with growing financial difficulties, the government attempted to float a loan abroad. Known as the "Berger Loan," from the name of one of the involved bankers, the amount was to be a million dollars. Although it was essential in order to save the country from bankruptcy, there was little support for the scheme in the National Assembly. As a result, Araujo resorted to a popular demonstration of support which he hoped would intimidate the legislature. On July 5 the Labor party faithful met at Campo Marte and marched to the president's palace. There, however, the demonstrators got out of hand. While expressing support for Araujo, they shouted for the ouster of Finance Minister Espinosa and Foreign Minister Reyes Arrieta-Rossi. Nevertheless, the demonstration convinced the legislature of the danger of anarchy, and the loan was approved. When word of this became known, the university students, led by AGEUS organizers such as the noncommunist Francisco Guillán Pérez, but also by the more inflammatory Alfonso Luna, met at the medical school of the university on July 11.

The Guardia Nacional was summoned to the scene, and its leader ordered the students to leave the medical school and

12. Durand, "Entrevista," *Diario Latino*, January 5, 1968.
13. N.A., R.G. 59, April 30, 1931, file 816.00/803.

disperse. They refused. Joaquín Castro Canizales, then teaching at the military academy, remembers arguing with the *guardia* leader, trying to persuade him not to use violence. But his pleas were useless; a bitter fight erupted between troops and students which resulted in numerous injuries and arrests.[14] The next day the government declared a state of siege. The official announcement in *La Prensa* on July 13 declared that it was "because of disorderly elements." Luis Felipe Recinos, who had earlier been repudiated by the president, was now made the censor of the press.

Araujo did make some tentative efforts toward helping the peasants. He persuaded the legislature to pass a law for the buying up of some land in the western departments of Santa Ana, La Libertad, Sonsonate, and San Salvador. These lands were divided carefully into small plots with access roads running between each to prevent them from being reconsolidated into large landholdings at a later date. They were then sold cheaply to the peasants. But there were too few parcels of land and too many *campesinos;* a hundred buyers presented themselves for each lot, and the experiment aroused discontent without doing much to help the masses of the people.[15]

On August 27 the newspapers in the capital announced an alarming new fall in world coffee prices. From that time on the economic situation was increasingly hopeless. On October 7 Araujo prohibited the export of gold, a move which annoyed and alarmed banking and financial circles. As a result, many bankers were afraid to grant the customary loans to coffee producers which were necessary to pay for harvest labor. Ultimately, much coffee rotted in the fields. When there was work, wages were miserably low. On November 11 *La Prensa* stated that growers were paying "fifteen centavos for each *tarea*" of coffee picked, plus two tortillas and a handful of beans. As this represented about a day's work, harvest wages had reached rock bottom. "It is painful," said the paper, "that

14. Marroquín, "Crisis," p. 49.
15. Such is the opinion of Serafín Quiteño, Marroquín, Castro Canizales, and other informed persons.

77

the landholders exploit the peasants in that manner. The authorities ought to investigate and correct these abuses." But, of course, the authorities could not work miracles.

The July 11 clash had marked the turning point for the government. From that time on it was totally in discredit. Abel Cuenca has summed up the situation as follows:

> Protest by the *campesinos* was now converted from isolated actions in the west of El Salvador...into a strike movement of strong and unheard of proportions. The government of Arturo Araujo, surprised by the crisis...was not prepared to counter the wave of incipient anarchy and vacillated before the blossoming mass movement between open repression and the application of legal, demagogic measures....The *cafetaleros* were alarmed and felt unsure of the fluctuating policy of the government, and soon they decided to replace Arturo Araujo with a more energetic president.[16]

This is a conspiratorial view of the coup of December 2. It makes it appear as though a vast secret network among the possessing classes and their military henchmen set out to seize power. Actually, there was probably little direct involvement of the *cafetaleros* in the events of December. There is no doubt, however, that they were unhappy and that they were in many cases close to the young officers who headed the movement. Besides sympathy with the economic plight of that class from which most of the officers of the army were drawn, there were many reasons why the military might have taken exception to the regime then in power. For corruption and inefficiency it was making a lasting name for itself. Further, it was not even able to meet the pay of the bureaucracy or the army. General Salvador Peña Trejo feels that the fact that the officers' pay was months in arrears had a good deal to do with the coup.[17]

16. Cuenca, *Democracia cafetalera*, pp. 31-32.
17. This information came out during our discussion of the coup. Peña Trejo was at the Escuela Militar and knew many of the conspirators personally.

But one cannot help suspecting that what really bothered many conservative military men was the socialistic aspect of the Labor party regime. There was the fear that somehow social reform might succeed in such a way as to make El Salvador a socialist country. Certainly, however, the army, whatever its motives, had the sympathy of the majority in the country, even among the poor.[18]

The tradition of the coup d'etat was deeply rooted in El Salvador, as throughout most of Latin America. It even had a certain "constitutional" justification in that the army considered itself the repository of the national will. According to this theory, the soldier's oath to preserve the country includes preserving it from bad civilian rulers. Military overthrows were (and still are) accomplished without anyone reflecting that the harm created by governmental instability and extralegal action is greater than that which could possibly, under any circumstances, be inflicted by the most disastrous constitutional regime.

The conspiracy began to gain momentum in November, 1931. On November 28 officers in the regiments stationed in the capital called for a brief strike to protest the lack of pay. That same day a young officer named Arístides R. Salazar called on General Salvador Castaneda Castro, El Salvador's foremost military figure, and asked him to assume leadership of a coup. He refused. Two days later Salazar visited him again. This time he brought with him Joaquín Castro Canizales, who was the real brains behind the conspiracy. (Although a very young man at the time, Castro Canizales was a prominent literary figure, in addition to being an influential instructor at the military school.) Again the general refused the conspirators. By the first of December there were rumors that the government was aware of the plot and that Araujo intended to transfer the officers involved to the provinces.

---

18. For the opposite view see Bustamante, *Historia militar*, p. 100. He says that "Violent political change was not generally pleasing, especially to the *campesinos*, because it ended his [Araujo's] promise to give them lands to work."

As a result, an emergency meeting of the conspirators was held at the Campo Marte on the north end of San Salvador, the site of what is now the children's park. This meeting took place on December 2 at 7:00 P.M. In addition to Salazar and Castro, Lt. Julio César Escobar and several other instructors from the military academy attended. As the Campo was too open they moved the meeting to the Escuela Padre Delgado.

Thirteen men attended this second meeting. They were told by the more informed conspirators that for the last four months a plot had been brewing in the first infantry barracks, next to the presidential palace (and on the site of what is now an outdoor market). The reason for immediate action was given as the forthcoming elections for *alcaldes*, or mayors of cities, across the country. In San Salvador, Araujo was backing a worker named Pedro Lázaro Meléndez, who was considered unacceptable to the military for the high post. The elections were scheduled for December 15 and the coup, it was explained, had originally been set for the thirteenth, but the rumored transfer of officers had forced the conspirators to move it up to this night, December 2.

Other events had also influenced the plotters to quicken their plan. On the morning of the second, rumor had swept the town that General Martínez was to be relieved of his position as minister of war. Araujo had called a meeting of his military staff at 4:00 P.M., and afterwards General Castaneda Castro, the director of the Escuela Militar, was seen deep in conversation with Col. Francisco Linares as they left the presidential palace. Col. Linares was the commanding officer of the first infantry barracks. This had further alarmed the conspirators who felt that the details of the plot might be known by the government,[19] and it stiffened their resolve to attempt the coup at once.

It might be well at this point to note the military situation of the capital. The city was ringed with barracks on all except the west and northwest side. The *caballeria*, or first cavalry, barracks lay to the northeast about three-quarters of a mile from the center of town. The sixth infantry barracks, occupied at

19. Quino Caso, "Insurrección militar," 1:3-5.

the time by the machine gun regiment, was half a mile southwest, in what is now the chief fire station. Due south and a little farther out lay "El Zapote," the most imposing of the fortifications. Its hill gave this barracks, which housed the artillery, perfect command of the city. The Policía Nacional, an organization roughly comparable to the state police in North America, but having responsibility as well for aiding urban police forces, had its headquarters downtown. Halfway between El Zapote and the center of town was the barracks of the Guardia Nacional, a rival of the *policía* and comparable to the Spanish Guardia Civil.[20] The first infantry, as mentioned above, was across the street and east of the presidential palace. Most of these barracks resembled the common notion of a medieval castle. They had high walls with gun slits in them, crenellated along the top. Watch towers stood at the corners. Barracks in the provinces were built the same way. Of course, such forts would be useless in modern warfare against an enemy with mortars and artillery, but they were not designed for fighting a regular army. Rather, the purpose of these forts, like those of many medieval lords, was to keep the populace in check. They were proof against men armed only with hand guns and machetes.

The "regiments" which occupied these imposing edifices were not comparable to European units of the same name, but were about the size of a modern company in numbers. At the time of the December 2, 1931, coup there were 120 men in the first infantry, about the same number in the artillery regiment, 30 men in the machine gunners, and similar small numbers in the units scattered around the country. In addition to forces at the capital, the nearby international airport at Ilopango had the government squadron of five twin-seater trainers.[21]

20. The *guardia* at this time was not considered a strictly military unit, although it was armed with rifles. It had existed since 1912 and was begun by a Spaniard, General Alfonso Martín Garrido, who patterned it on the Spanish Guardia Civil. The *policía* was generally referred to at this time as the Policía de Línea, today Policía Nacional. Both the *guardia* and the police were elite units, being much better paid than the army. An army private made fifty centavos a day and a *guardia* private three times that amount. There were a total of about 3,500 in the two organizations.
21. Quino Caso, "Insurrección militar," 3: 4; 4: 3; 6: 4.

San Salvador in 1932

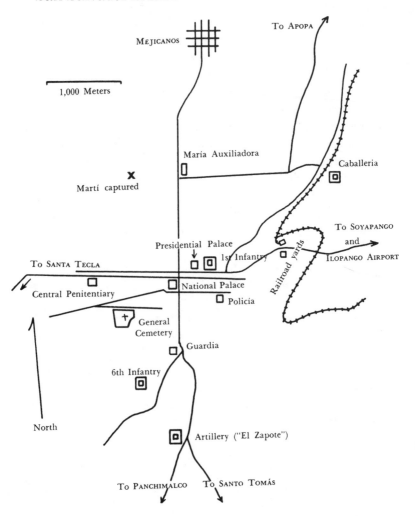

1,000 Meters

MEJICANOS

To APOPA

María Auxiliadora

X
Martí captured

Caballeria

To SOYAPANGO
and
ILOPANGO AIRPORT

Presidential Palace

1st Infantry

Railroad yards

To SANTA TECLA

National Palace

Central Penitentiary

Policía

General
Cemetery

Guardia

6th Infantry

North

Artillery ("El Zapote")

To PANCHIMALCO   To SANTO TOMÁS

At 9:30 in the evening, Castro Canizales, Escobar, and Arístides Salazar entered the headquarters of the first infantry. There they were joined by Captain Eugenio Palma, an officer of the regiment. He had alerted some of the men in the barracks who were loyal to himself. All that now remained was to arrest the senior officers. They went first for Col. Coronado Montalvo, the second in command, who was captured at gunpoint and led into the library. At that moment, more of the conspirators came into the room and he seized the opportunity to shout, "Mi *colonel, auxiliooo…*" at which point a hand was clamped on his mouth and he was subdued. But Col. Linares, who was nearby, heard the noise and immediately called the presidential palace next door to inform the guards that something was going on in his barracks. At that moment he was seized, but the president had already been alerted.[22] In the artillery barracks, a similar scene was being enacted. There Col. Santiago Ayala went for his gun when the conspirators entered. Shots were exchanged and he was gravely wounded. This action also helped alert the city.

The next hour was spent in hurried preparation for the assault on the president's palace. At 11:00 P.M. the attack was launched, but it was stoutly repulsed by the soldiers and police on duty there. A second wave of assault troops, striking at midnight, fared no better. In the face of this check, the insurrectionists brought up machine guns and began to rain ammunition into the palace. These weapons were in their hands because the sixth infantry barracks had likewise fallen. In the confusion, however, Don Arturo Araujo escaped his battered official residence. He went first to his own home, where he attempted to summon support, and then, at 1:00 A.M., to the Palacio Nacional, which is on the central square of the city a few blocks from the site of the old presidential palace. There he organized his defense of the city against the rebels. The cavalry regiment was loyal, and a cordon of troopers was thrown around the building. From their rival headquarters, the two groups sniped at each other, while the cavalry attempted to patrol the

22. Ibid., 4: 1.

streets and drive the rebels into their barracks. The *policía* and the *guardia* at first aided the troopers.

At 5:00 in the morning, the fortunes of war began to change. A third attack against the presidential palace succeeded in breaking through stout resistance, despite the fact that the leader of the charge, Lt. Mariano Blanco, was killed. About the same time, the *guardia* went over to the revolutionaries. The cavalry and the police, now hopelessly outnumbered and virtually surrounded, agreed to surrender shortly thereafter.

In the meantime, the conspirators had been busy in El Zapote where Joaquín Castro Canizales and the other ringleaders had gone after the first attacks on the president's residence. They formed a military civilian directorate which was to govern the country until some ultimate disposition could be made. The chief "civilian" was Castro himself; although he was a teacher at the military school, he held no official rank at the time. Later on, Martínez made him a lieutenant. At El Zapote, the new junta received a call from Charles Boyd Curtiss, the new American minister, who had replaced Warren D. Robbins in October. He asked if they would receive a diplomatic delegation. They agreed, and at 6:00 A.M. Curtiss himself arrived at El Zapote. Learning that a junta had been formed, he offered his "good offices" to go to the other barracks and inform them of the situation. To that the rebels agreed. Curtiss not only drove around the capital and talked to the men at the other barracks, but he then brought delegates from those *cuarteles* to talk with the junta in El Zapote.[23]

While this was going on, Araujo had fled to his parents' home on the Santa Tecla road at, ironically enough, the site of the present Escuela Militar. From there he tried to rally his forces. The director general of the *policía* was Major Salvador López Rochac, Don Arturo's brother-in-law, and presumably a man he could trust. As it happened, this functionary was in Sonsonate when the coup occurred. He and General Miguel Mora Castro, commander of the Sonsonate regiment, were attempting to march on the capital.[24] Araujo decided to join

23. Ibid., 5: 3-4; 7: 1
24. Bustamente, *Historia militar*, p. 106.

them, but before he left, he decided to put in a call to El Zapote. When he announced to the man who answered who he was, another person was immediately put on the phone. It was General Maximiliano Hernández Martínez, the vice-president and minister of war. Arturo Araujo felt a sudden elation. Perhaps El Zapote had fallen to loyal troops and the rebellion had been crushed.

"What are you doing there?" he asked.

"I am a prisoner," General Martínez replied.

Don Arturo was stunned. He hung up, still wondering how it was that a "prisoner" was answering the phone.[25]

General Martínez, according to what he later told Castro Canizales, was asleep when he received a call from Arturo Araujo on the night of December 2 saying that something strange was going on at the first infantry barracks. He dressed at once and ordered his son, Alberto, to call for his car. They left their house, across from the Asilio Sara, and had the driver take them to the *Edificio Ambrogi* downtown. They went up to the top of the building to take a good look over the city. Hearing firing and seeing the seriousness of the situation, they drove at once to El Zapote.

As soon as the car came in range it was fired on by machine guns from the barracks. Weaving up the road, they managed to bring the car in close to the wall, below the angle at which a gun could be depressed. Here they ran into a certain Col. Espínosa, wandering around aimlessly in the dark. He explained the barracks was in rebel hands and he did not know what to do. Disgusted, Martínez marched up to the big iron door and banged on it with the butt of his pistol, demanding that they open up for the minister of war. Lt. Cañas, who was at the door, had the presence of mind to open it, and the general stepped inside. There he was promptly seized and disarmed. His son and the driver were also taken.[26]

Such is the story of General Martínez. Needless to say, Arturo Araujo never believed it. In his last interview he declared: "It was General Martínez who secretly directed the

25. Durand, "Entrevista," *Diario Latino*, January 5, 1968.
26. Quino Caso, "Insurrección militar," 4: 4-5.

movement which brought him to power....I do not believe that other members of my government, honorable men, were involved."[27] Abel Cuenca, and most other Salvadorean leftists that I have talked to, agree that the general must have been in on the plot. It is quite evident, from the not very exalted rank of the ostensible leaders, that they must have been counting on support in high places when they attempted the revolt.

However, after talking with Joaquín Castro Canizales several times, I feel certain that he is being quite truthful when he asserts that, to his knowledge, General Martínez was not aware of the impending coup, although he knew that there was grave dissatisfaction and that many officers were conspiring against the regime. General Salvador Peña Trejo has suggested that Martínez was not aware of the details of any one plot, but was fully aware that *something* was in the wind, and was ready to profit by whatever occurred. This seems to me to be about as close to the truth as it is now possible to come.

North American pressure had much to do with the eventual installation of the former vice-president as ruler of the country. In his negotiations with the junta, Curtiss explained that, in view of the agreement which the United States had with the Central American States not to recognize any government brought to power by a coup, it would be impossible for the United States to accept them as the legally constituted authority, especially as the Salvadorean constitution made no provision for a multiple executive. Their best hope, he went on, was to pull the cloak of legality over the whole proceedings by installing some acceptable representative of the prior regime, such as the vice-president, until new elections would be held and a real civilian regime appointed.[28]

At the close of the coup, the young men who had ostensibly planned it had given away to more experienced officers. The real leaders of the junta were now two colonels: Joaquín Valdés, who became minister of war under Martínez, and Osmín Aguirre y Salinas, who was made chief of police. Behind them, at least according to Curtiss, was the shadowy figure of

27. Durand, "Entrevista," *Diario Latino*, January 5, 1968.
28. Quino Caso, "Insurrección militar," 7: 1.

Rodolfo Duke, the leading personage in Banco Agrícola Comercial and a hard, calculating man who had presidential aspirations for himself.[29]

These leaders approached General Martínez, still a prisoner in El Zapote, and he accepted the task of becoming provisional chief of state. The junta continued for eight days more and finally dissolved itself on December 10, whereupon most of its members stepped into lucrative jobs in the new administration. Their haste in setting up a quasi-legal government was due to the insistence of the U.S. minister and that of our top Latin American troubleshooter, Jefferson Caffery, who had hurriedly flown to El Salvador from his post in Colombia when the trouble started.[30]

It was chiefly the speed with which all this was accomplished that led observers to believe that the vice-president could not but have had a hand in the revolt itself. Certainly, by accident or design, things had fallen his way. Joaquín Castro Canizales and his group had served as front men for Osmín Aguirre and Valdés, and perhaps for Rodolfo Duke, and it appeared not unlikely that behind them was the noted theosophist himself, who, within the space of twenty-four hours, had passed from prisoner to provisional president. At any rate, it was mistakenly assumed that Martínez would use his powers to call new elections sometime in early 1932. The revolt of January, however, gave him ample pretext for failing to meet these expectations and for staying on for two more years, after which he gave way briefly, only to return as dictator and remain in office until 1944, ruling the country with a blend of shrewdness and mysticism.

In the meantime, the unfortunate legal president of the country, Don Arturo Araujo, had been persuaded on the third of

29. N.A., R.G. 59, C.B. Curtiss to Secretary of State, December 17, 1931, File 816.00/811. Duke was one of the bankers dissatisfied with the Berger Loan and the economic policies of Araujo.
30. Quino Caso, "Insurrección militar," 7: 1. Caffery was familiar with El Salvador's politics, having been stationed there in the twenties. On the fifth he flew on to Washington, giving the impression that he was going to plead for recognition. His failure to persuade Washington to recognize the new government was a great disappointment in El Salvador.

December to shift his headquarters from Santa Tecla, just southwest of the capital, to Santa Ana in the northwest. By the next day his attempts to rally his forces had failed and the leading members of the government, including Araujo himself and Luis Felipe Recinos, sought asylum in Guatemala. Oddly enough, Jorge Ubico, the new ruler of Guatemala, was a close personal friend of Arturo Araujo, although Ubico was a typical "strongman" type of ruler and Araujo a sincere liberal. Araujo tried to use the friendship to regain power in El Salvador. He made injudicious statements to the press of his plans for a counterrevolution; there were rumors that he planned to bomb San Salvador. This threat was constantly played up in the Salvadorean papers during the first two months that General Martínez was in power, and it aided him in maintaining the state of emergency which was his excuse for retaining office. Eventually, Ubico became so embarrassed by the presence of the former president of El Salvador that he forced him to leave for Honduras. Araujo never reentered Salvadorean politics, but watched from exile the tragic series of events which now unfolded in his homeland.

Chapter 5

Martí Organizes the Masses

The period of Araujo's election campaign and his brief presidency coincides with increased propaganda and agitation by the extreme left, a fact which had much to do with the president's inability to retain office. Thus it is pertinent to turn to the story of the radicals, and the man who was heart and soul of the movement, Agustín Farabundo Martí.

At the beginning of summer, 1930, Martí returned to El Salvador. Because he had been a fighter in Sandino's army, he enjoyed considerable prestige, despite the fact that he was now denouncing Sandino as a member of the bourgeoisie and a false prophet. He also returned with the support of the SRI headquarters in New York. Soon after he arrived in the country he became secretary-general of the Central Committee of the SRI in El Salvador. It was from this position that he directed the activities of the extremists. If he held a similar position in the Communist party there is no record of it, but the party was closely allied to the SRI.

A series of workers' and peasants' protests against depression conditions, and incidentally, in favor of the Soviet Union, in early August led to the August 12 decrees of the Pío Romero Bosque government and the jailing of hundreds of demonstrators. Martí and the SRI then sprang into action.[1] They not only collected money and food for the prisoners and their families, but also saw to it that the imprisonment received the widest possible publicity both at home and abroad. Such activity did not endear Martí to the government. He was

1. [Arias Gómez], Martí, p. 13.

89

arrested on several occasions, the last time on November 27 in Santa Ana. On that occasion Don Pío decided that it would be wisest to get the famous agitator out of the country until after the presidential elections were held.

According to a letter from Martí himself,[2] it was on the night of December 19 that a government official named Carlos Valdés visited Martí in his cell. He brought with him paper, pen, and ink and urged the prisoner to write a note to the director of the *policía* asking for a passport from the country. "My response," Martí recalled, "was that he, his idea, and those writing things ought to get out of my cell." Valdés then left to inform the government that the prisoner would not voluntarily petition for exile. The next day the director of the police came to ask Martí if he would be willing to try the climate of Panama. The prisoner responded again that he could be made to leave only by force. The policeman shrugged his shoulders. Very well, force it would have to be. That night Martí was hauled from his cell. Twelve dollars were stuffed into his pocket along with a steamship ticket. At La Libertad he was put aboard the steamer *Venezuela* the next morning.

The ship's captain, Walter N. Prengel, had been given to understand that the prisoner was a dangerous character and had been paid to take him well away from Central America. When the tramp steamer touched at Guatemalan ports the next few days, Martí was kept locked up below decks. By the time they reached Mexico the captain had been persuaded by the prisoner to let him attempt to land, but the Mexican government had been forewarned, and wanted no part of the famous communist. Unlike Trotsky, who later received asylum there, Martí was not a fallen and discredited leader, but an active political force whose intended revolution would be a little too close to home.

In California he managed to get off the ship, but got no further than the office of immigration, where he remained from New Year's Eve to the twelfth of January. Locked up in San Pedro, he received visits from a number of local leftists, but their sympathy alone was not enough to secure his release; when

2. Luna, "Vida de Martí," pp. 101-6.

the *Venezuela* upped anchor on January 12, Martí was again a passenger. They worked their way back down the coast, Martí again being locked up while in Guatemalan ports. However, on arrival in La Libertad, the captain told him he might leave, as his orders were only to hold him until after the elections and they had now been held. He was no sooner off the ship than government agents, who had been expecting him, put him on board again.

At last, in Punta Arenas, Costa Rica, the new "man without a country" was allowed ashore. An agent of the Salvadorean government was waiting with $28.00 in cash and a new steamboat ticket, this time to Peru. Put aboard the tramp steamer *Colombia* at Balboa, he jumped ship at Corinto, Nicaragua. He arrived in the town of Chinandega on February 2 and remained there until the middle of the month. He probably received funds from the Salvadorean communists, which allowed him to slip first into Honduras and from there into El Salvador. It was not until the twentieth of the month that he found himself in San Salvador, ready to take up his leadership of the SRI again. The public and the government were not long unaware of his return. On February 25 a letter to the editors of *La Prensa* from Sr. Rafael A. Salinas warned that the leading red agitator was back in town.

Already there was plenty of discontent to work with. On Saturday, January 24, the papers announced that there was strong communist activity in Armenia, led by Gregorio Cortés Cordero, a former judge. They also reported communist-inspired rallies in San Isidro and Izalco.

Martí rested by his ocean voyage, was ready to resume his leadership role. Throughout the course of events from his return in February, 1931, until his execution in February, 1932, he displayed remarkable coolness, the fatalistic calm of a man who knew that whatever his personal destiny might be, the movement he led would eventually triumph. "I do not wish to defend myself," he told his judges at the trial that condemned him to death, "because my work and that of my comrades will be justified."[3]

3. Pineda, "Tragedia comunista," *Diario de Hoy*, January 20, 1967.

Geography gave the propagandists a definite advantage. El Salvador was small and accessible enough to be propagandized from a single central headquarters. Further, it was close enough to Guatemala to facilitate international contacts and far enough from the United States to prevent immediate interference. Still, it is estimated that the work of the radicals did not touch the lives of most people in El Salvador. At the height of Martí's activity, 75 percent of the population were completely apathetic politically. This was especially true in the more thinly populated eastern zone.[4] The activities of Martí and his followers mostly covered the area from Lake Ilopango westward to the border and from the city of Santa Ana southward to the sea.

The decision to propagandize the masses of the peasantry was a crucial one for the extreme left. Up until the last year of Don Pio's regime, FRTS had been concentrating upon the small numbers of artisans and service employees in the major centers, but the success of Jorge Fernandéz Anaya demonstrated the possibility of rural support. Now, with Martí and Fernández Anaya (who left El Salvador in the spring of 1931) both on the scene, it was inevitable that a vast campaign to organize rural labor would be undertaken.

Propaganda among largely illiterate masses of people runs into definite problems unless one has access to a radio station, which, of course, the agitators did not. There were two main methods of disseminating information. One was the "popular university," a kind of teach-in, at which students from the university in the capital would come out into the provincial towns and lecture the peasants and workers on economics, agriculture, history, and inevitably, politics. Martí, although a poor public speaker, is said by many to have participated. These groups were prominent in Ahuachapán, Izalco, Juayúa, and other centers in western El Salvador. A second method was to make use of the village schoolmasters, who often became agents of the radical movement. Often only half-educated themselves, they accepted the rather facile ideas drawn up by SRI, FRTS, or the Communist party with little question. In

4. Jorge Schlesinger, *Revolución comunista*, pp. 10-11.

Machón Vilanova's novel *Ola Roja*, the heroine, María Gertrudis, is one of these propagandist-teachers. Among the points in her program are: (1) nationalization of the means of transport and communication; (2) equal opportunities for women; (3) a thirty-six hour week; (4) unionization and the right of the peasants to strike; (5) security against unemployment for ill health, maternity, and old age, plus minimum wages; (6) free, universal education; (7) cultivation of all available lands; (8) progressive taxation; (9) an end to the Indian caste system. The last seemed to the novelist an important point. The Indians "know that the white conqueror...forced them to submit to obedience and servitude. But they have not forgotten these old grievances nor lost their bravery or their hope."[5] This list of goals tallies pretty well with others which I heard from those who remembered the movement.

One of the most ingenious ideas that the propagandists came up with was the use of illustrative drawings. The pictures, crude in draftsmanship and far too complicated to convey a clear idea, were still useful memory reinforcers when used in conjunction with oral lectures. They remind one of the rough brown-paper drawings still used in El Salvador by rural health workers and Peace Corps volunteers to illustrate their points. The earlier pictures showed the local patrician class as linked to a vast capitalist conspiracy headed by Washington politicos or by Wall Street. Here Uncle Sam was pictured surrounded by his diplomatic gunboats, sending out orders to vast legions of United Fruit Company agents throughout Central America. The United States and world capitalism were made to take the blame for low coffee prices which resulted from the Great Depression, and, with less justice, were made responsible for the bad government of El Salvador.[6]

Any occasion could serve as a chance to work among the people. The supposedly miraculous appearance of the "Virgen del Adelanto" near Ahuachapán brought many nonreligious

5. Machón Vilanova, *Ola roja*, pp. 326, 353-54.
6. Jorge Schlesinger, in *Revolución comunista*, pp. 139-42, includes several photos of these crude pictures.

pilgrims to the scene to preach their "evangelism of death."[7] Agents of the radical left frequently disguised themselves as peddlers or traveling salesmen. In El Salvador at that time it was generally assumed by the populace, who traditionally despised this kind of commerce, that most peddlers were foreigners, generally "Turcos"—Levantines from Syria, Lebanon, or even Armenia. Others were classified as "Slavs" or "Jews," often with little foundation other than color or accent. This attitude had given rise to the curious belief that vast numbers of foreign infiltrators had worked their way into the country to spread communism. Such men were, presumably, paid in Moscow; the journalist Alfredo Schlesinger went so far as to say that the revolt in El Salvador was directed "by orders from Moscow."[8]

As evidence of foreign involvement, a document can be shown from the SRI in New York, dated February 26, 1931, advising the executive committee of the SRI in El Salvador that: "We have just received the enclosed letter which advises us that beginning in January of this year you will receive economic aid of fifty dollars which will be sent by us. We believe that the first three monthly payments will be received in March and as soon as we receive them we will send them on." The letter is signed R. Gómez.[9] Certainly however, the sum mentioned is a trifle. It is doubtful that Martí and his friends received much foreign aid. In view of his maverick tendencies, and perhaps "Trotskyite" leanings, he was probably not on particularly good terms with Moscow-oriented communists; the revolt was largely a home-grown product.

As for the "foreign infiltrators," there was and is a widespread antipathy in El Salvador between the Spanish-Indian inhabitants and the Turcos, due in large part to the hard work of the latter, and their ability to rise in commerce.

7. "Lt. Flores Narrative," in Pineda, "Tragedia comunista," Diario de Hoy, February 2, 1967.
8. Alfredo Schlesinger, La verdad sobre el comunismo, 2d ed. (Guatemala, 1932) p. 100. The chargé at the time, Jefferson Caffery, speaks of two Russians expelled in 1927 for having made communist propoganda (N.A., R.G. 59, August 24, 1927, file 816.00B/3).
9. Jorge Schlesinger, Revolución comunista, p. 213.

Anything bad might be believed about the Turcos. As for "Slavic" infiltrators, the chances of large numbers of them trooping through the Salvadorean countryside stirring up trouble seem most remote. On the other hand, all these rumors appear not to have been entirely without foundation.

Col. José Asencio Menéndez tells me that, when he was an exchange officer serving with the French army in 1930, a former White Russian officer showed him photos of a Pole, a Czech, and a Russian who were in El Salvador disguised as peddlers but were really there to make propaganda. This information he, of course, relayed to the government. Further, Martínez's chief of the *policía*, Col. Osmín Aguirre y Salinas, has written for me a brief account in which he mentions that there were "five or six Polish or Yugoslav peddlers" going about the country selling religious goods cheaply or on credit in order to give them a chance to propagandize. On the night the revolt began, his agents caught several of them near the Basílica de Guadalupe, in the act of cutting the telegraph lines between the capital and Santa Tecla. They were killed by his police. Col. Aguirre is not the sort to imagine "foreign infiltrator" if there were none. Another item indicating external influences is a document which was captured after the revolt, and which was included in the personal papers of the chief of the National Police. It suggests the use of Arabic as a code among the radicals, indicating, perhaps, a high number of Turcos among them.[10]

While Indianism may not have played a large part in the success of communist propaganda throughout all of the western zone, in the intensely Indian districts of Sonsonate it was extremely important. That was why one of the most important converts to the new doctrine was the cacique of Izalco, José Feliciano Ama. Ama had a strong hold over the *barrio* of Asunción, the Indian *barrio* of the town, through his chieftainship and through his leadership in the *cofradía*. He had inherited this position of power from his father-in-law, Patricio Shupan. Shupan had long looked after the external affairs of the Indian community and was a definite force in Salvadorean politics. He

10. Osmín Aguirre collection. This was dated March 18, 1932 and was from A.C. Bendeke to Neftali Lagos in Tegucigalpa.

had been wooed by Quiñónez Molina and had aided the crafty leader of Liga Roja in his election campaign. For this Shupan had been rewarded with even greater authority. However, in 1924, shortly after a dinner at the presidential palace in San Salvador, Shupan fell ill and died. Rumor, probably false, had it that the president had poisoned him, a belief which in turn helped poison Indian-Ladino relations. The president's lavish state funeral for the fallen chieftain only increased suspicion. Why should he waste such attention on an Indian unless he had something to hide?

In the space of the next three years Ama, Shupan's son-in-law, consolidated his position as cacique, with the aid of his devoted lieutenant Félix Turish. Local estimates of Ama's wealth vary greatly, but tradition has it that he was not a poor man. He may have been worth forty thousand colones. He was said to have been hard working and intelligent. During the election campaign of 1930 he swung the weight of his prestige behind Alberto Gómez Zárate. This meant that he could expect little from Araujo's government and may have made him more receptive to left-wing propaganda. At any rate, he was visited by several agents of the extremists, probably led by Miguel Mármol. They convinced him of the certain triumph of the communist cause.

To the Indians of the Izalco region, the fact that these Reds were linked to an international movement must have greatly enhanced their status. They were believed to be the possessors of some sort of secret weapon or magic which would allow their triumph. Hugo Granadino, the historian of Sonsonate, tells me that when his father tried to warn some of the Indians not to participate in the doomed movement they laughed at him, saying that the soldiers would shoot balls of corn meal in their guns rather than bullets when they faced the communists.

Then too, the racial appeal must have been important. Ama, despite all his power, was still a despised Indio in the eyes of the citizens of Barrio Dolores. The communist promise to humble the Ladino and elevate the Indian must have had an appeal not unlike that of "black power" in the United States in the 1960s. When, in mid-1931, Ama was warned in a letter from

Gómez Zárate that he was making a mistake, he replied, "I do not want to have correspondence with an arrogant and exploitative bourgeois."[11] One can hardly imagine that he chose this language himself. The other Indian leaders in Izalco and the surrounding area, many of them men of property like Ama, were attracted, also like Ama, primarily by the hope of political office. Francisco Sánchez, the leading figure among the Indians of Juayúa and the actual, though not official, cacique, was promised the mayorship of that town. The cacique of Nahuizalco received a similar promise.

Certain Ladinos also were taken in. Around Sonsonate the most prominent was Eusebio Chávez, a fifty-two-year-old carpenter, and his son Leopoldo. They both lived in Barrio Dolores. Eusebio had been politically active and was defeated by Miguel Call in his bid to become *alcalde* of Izalco just before the 1932 revolt. In Tacuba, much farther to the west, the prominent Cuenca brothers were deeply involved in radical activity. They were merchants in the town and were said to own the pharmacy and the inn as well as some land. Several were university students, and the most brilliant, Abel, had received radical ideas at the University of Guatemala.

In addition to their rural work in western El Salvador, the men of the extreme left began an intense drive among the university students in the capital. Today, popular mythology among the middle class in El Salvador has it that the university is now filled with "communists," meaning those desiring some changes in the antiquated social structure of the country. Even in the late twenties university students had a reputation for radicalism, but in fact, propaganda among them was the seed sown on rocky ground. The university students had been dissatisfied with the Quiñónez-Meléndez group and they longed for a more liberal administration, but this hardly made them communists. Actually, their vague radicalism made it extremely difficult to propagandize among them. They were, as Abel Cuenca says, "all passion and no action." Men like Martí,

11. Pineda, "Tragedia comunista," *Diario de Hoy*, February 4, 1967; Jorge Schlesinger, *Revolución comunista*, pp. 25-26. Gómez Zárate was the local victor in Izalco, thanks to the efforts of Feliciano Ama.

although drawn from the student ranks, quickly became isolated when they embraced communism.

Only three members of the younger generation of students played important roles in the 1932 revolt. They were Alfonso Luna, Mario Zapata, and Inocente Rivas Hidalgo. These men may have met Martí on his visit to the country just before his Sandino venture, but they did not start working with him until the fall of 1930.

Alfonso Luna was from Ahuachapán, where he is still well remembered. He was the son of Don Eduardo Luna and María (or Marí) Calderón de Luna. His parents are described as having been hardworking people, well thought of in the community. Both of these parents were dead by the end of the twenties, and Alfonso lived when at home with his grandmother, Idalecia Luna. Judging from his pictures he was quite dark complexioned, and rather heavy faced, although he is remembered as having been fairly tall and very thin. With his Indian features and his straight black hair combed back over his head, he looked considerably older than his twenty-one years.

His family had been landholders, and although not terribly wealthy they had been able to send him to be educated at the Liceo San Luis in Santa Ana and then to the university. Both in his secondary school and at the university he was regarded as an extremely brilliant student. In 1929 he began radical activity, not as a communist but rather as a supporter of a Salvadorean APRA group. However, he got to know Martí when the latter returned from his exploits with Sandino, and was soon a follower of the SRI leader.

Mario Zapata, slightly younger than Luna, was a thin-faced, bespectacled youth. Although most agree that he was not as brilliant a scholar as Luna, he was known as the more passionate of the two. He was the son of Doña Mercedes Zapata. His father's family had been prominent in politics. His uncle, Dr. Baltazar Zapata, was at one time the governor of San Miguel.[12] According to a boyhood friend of Zapata, his parents were divorced and an unhappy homelife had contributed greatly to his distaste for bourgeois existence. His mother later

12. Many of these details are found in *Diario Latino*, February 1, 1932.

married Dr. Franciso Gutiérrez, the consul general of Nicaragua.

Inocente Rivas Hidalgo, who played a less prominent part in the revolt and managed to escape execution, was also highly connected in Salvadorean politics. He was a close companion of Luna and Zapata. Perhaps because of their pathetic execution, most commentators are inclined to view Luna and Zapata in a favorable light. Jorge Schlesinger, in his otherwise anticommunist tract, displays a marked sympathy for them, seeing them as idealistic youngsters, influenced by religious convictions that made them want to come to the aid of the poor, even if it meant joining an organization which the church condemned.[13]

Rodolfo Buezo, the secretary of Alfredo Schlesinger, paints a similar picture in his sympathetic account of the revolution. "Their ideas," he says, "did not differ much from those of their fellows, but, being acute observers of the way things were, of the political forces and social organizations of the country and seeing the struggle of the Communist party led by A. F. Martí, they fixed their attention on that chaotic state of social injustice and from this sprang their enthusiasm for the agrarian anti-Imperialist movement."

Buezo claimed that, before his execution, Zapata expressed his ideas in a series of conversations with one of his judges. If these third-hand recollections can be trusted they paint a picture of an extremely enthusiastic and loyal young man. In these memoirs Zapata insisted that he had originally been apolitical. "My last years in the baccalaureate program passed without strong emotions. In those days, when party passions were agitating the country, I shied away from those partisans who revealed a mixture of personal ambition and petty fetishism.... These political struggles did not interest me. I always had for politics a veritable repugnance because it was not a contest of ideas."

But being from a very wealthy family, Zapata had little chance for first-hand observation of the true lot of the poor. When he first learned of the injustices in the country, from such

13. Jorge Schlesinger, *Revolución comunista*, pp. 46-47.

men as José Luis Barrientos and Farabundo Martí, he resisted believing them. Little by little he began to learn for himself. On vacations, he took to visiting *the fincas* of wealthy friends to find out what he could about social conditions. At one hacienda, "they employed more than four hundred men....On Saturday they paid them, but very little remained because a part was left at the tavern owned by the *finca* and the rest at the company store....It was my first bad impression." At another house of a friend he found the table richly laid for lunch with beer, chicken, and meats. He thought it was for the lunch of the *hacendado* and his family, but then some *guardia* came in and fell to. On asking about this he was told: "They are our salvation, without the *guardia* we could not operate."[14]

After becoming activists, Luna and Zapata served on the editorial board of *Opinión Estudiantil,* then as now the student newspaper of the University of El Salvador. It was not at any time during this period a "communist" publication. Indeed, the strongest voice among the student editors was Francisco Guillán Pérez, who organized the great medical school demonstration against Araujo. During the election campaign of 1930 the student paper had supported the "most bourgeois of the candidates," Dr. Enrique Córdova.[15] In general, the paper was sympathetic to Martí, especially after his hunger strike in the spring of 1931 when he became a national hero, but it was far from endorsing any revolution. For this reason, late in 1931, Luna and Zapata formed their own newspaper, *Estrella Roja,* named for the famous paper of the Soviet Army. Volume one, number one is dated December 12, 1931, or after the Martínez coup. The paper was published only twice before being suppressed.

The official Communist party publication was *Verdad (Pravda),* and Inocente Rivas Hidalgo was on its editorial staff. René Padilla Velasco, who defended Martí in his final trial, suggests that there were about a dozen extreme leftists in all among the university students. He and most others agree that even these young idealists were not "communists" in the strict

14. Buezo, *Sangre de hermanos*, pp. 10, 13.
15. Jorge Schlesinger, *Revolución comunista*, pp. 53-54.

sense of the word; it is doubtful if they were actually party members. Further, in regard to the supposed leadership of Luna and Zapata, most persons familiar with the revolt agree that any leadership they showed was a moral one. They were not directors of the movement. Joaquín Castro Canizales remembers that at the trial of Martí, Luna, and Zapata after the revolt, the SRI leader said that his two student companions had not been leaders; that they were not even true communists because they had not ceased to be members of the possessing class. They had received no indoctrination and had not undergone sufficient trials to develop true proletarian convictions. In taking the blame, and downgrading the importance of his followers, Martí was trying to spare them from execution, but most other informed observers agreed with him.[16]

When Martí returned from his enforced ocean voyage in February, 1931, he was determined to stir up trouble. The poor prices on the world market for coffee had led to a decline in the number of harvest jobs available from November to February, and when there was work, the pay was very poor. Naturally, the SRI leader took advantage of the discontent this caused. On March 21 the papers in the capital spoke of widespread disturbances of the peace. La Prensa noted that these had been growing since February 25—in short, since Martí returned. On March 20 there was a huge rally at the Parque Barrios, in front of the National Palace. When ordered to disperse, the mob refused and troops under the command of Col. Salvador López were called in to rout them from the park. The manifesto of those organizing the rally was reprinted in the papers. Attacking capitalism in general and the coffee culture in particular, it complained of widespread hunger and misery.

These disturbances in the capital were followed on Sunday, March 22, by equally severe clashes in Santa Ana, where it was believed that Martí was present. In response to the growing disorder of February and March, the Araujo government put into effect what a communist circular of the time called "the fascist law," giving army and police units greater power in

16. An exception is López Vallecillos, in *El periodismo*, p 155.

putting down strikes and demonstrations.[17] Inspired by this legislation, the police began a series of raids against leftist headquarters and began to search the mail to pull from it subversive documents. Around April 1 the government discovered great quantities of communist literature in the mails with instructions for new and more violent attempts to organize the workers and peasants. Much of this literature came from SRI headquarters in New York.

Angered by the seizure, Martí led a march on the president's own house, where he spoke before the crowd, insulting the president to his ears if not his face. With that provocation, the government arrested Martí and his follower Rafael Bondanza on April 9. Officially, he was charged with inciting the March 20 riot at Parque Barrios, and was lodged in the Central Penitentiary in San Salvador.

On April 29 the government announced that it had evidence of an "alliance of Communists and politicos," presumably for a coup. Araujo promised "firm action," and the government congratulated itself on having discovered the plot in time. Meanwhile, Martí imprisoned was proving a greater embarrassment than Martí at large. On Tuesday, May 5, he launched his famous hunger strike. Government attempts to keep this a secret failed, and on the eleventh it was announced in the papers. By May 20 his condition had deteriorated to the point that he was transferred from the prison to the Hospital Rosales. In the meantime, pressure was building up for his release. Whether the arrest of Martí was the chief cause of the discontent or whether, as Gustavo Pineda suggests, the cause was the inept regime of Araujo,[18] it is certain that the kettle was now boiling.

Sonsonate was the center of these new disturbances. A series of clashes in that town between police and demonstrators led to a massacre on May 17 in which a number of workers and peasants were killed. The fighting was provoked by the policies of the governor of Sonsonate, Arístides Castillo, who was known

17. Osmín Aguirre collection.
18. Pineda, "Tragedia comunista," *Diario de Hoy*, January 17, 1967.

to be extremely hostile to the FRTS.[19] The same day a meeting protesting Martí imprisonment was broken up in the capital.

On May 18 peasants led by an agitator named Manuel Mojica (evidently an Indio) poured into Sonsonate from Izalco, Nahuizalco, and Sonzacate, in a foretaste of the great revolt. Again, troops and *guardia* were called out and "blood flowed," as the papers put it. The radicals lost no time in exploiting these incidents. A manifesto which appeared in Sonsonate around this time stated:

> Workers, peasants and soldiers. The mass assassination of workers and peasants in Sonsonate was ordered and executed by the fascist government of Arturo Araujo. The Communist Party of El Salvador denounces the government of Arturo Araujo as a government of assassins and animals and calls all the poor workers and peasants of the world to solidarity with their brothers in El Salvador....The Communist Party calls all the poor workers and peasants of El Salvador to bloody struggle against the national bourgeoisie, who are unconditionally allied to Yankee Imperialists.... Down with the imperialist oppressor and his national dogs! Down with the fascist government of Arturo Araujo! *Viva* the Communist Party of El Salvador.[20]

Shortly after the affair in Sonsonate, a similar incident in Zaragoza resulted in twelve dead and thirty-three injured on the side of the peasants and several wounded among the forces of the government. All of this served to alarm the government; General José Tomás Calderón had been sent out in May to report on conditions in Sonsonate. His report, dated May 18,

---

19. Luna, "Tragico suceso," pp. 57-60. Twenty-three persons lost their lives in these Sonsonate disturbances.
20. Jorge Schlesinger, *Revolución comunista*, pp. 142-43.

gives us the view that the government must have had of these events.[21]

> To the President of the Republic:
>
> More than two hours of conference with the governor and the director of police cause me to believe it is necessary that directives be issued immediately to guarantee public order against possible communist reaction, given the aggressiveness of a mob of eight hundred to a thousand men and their ostentatious disrespect and lack of fear of authority....It is necessary that the garrison be reinforced by a section of machine gunners, with two pieces and four thousand rounds.... It is also necessary to add twenty police agents to the regular police....I have talked with two leaders among the prisoners and they are so radical about their erroneous theories that they have allowed them to be translated into aggressive action on the part of their followers.

A second letter, dated from the capital on May 22, completes the view that the general wished to give his superiors.

> I have the honor to present you the following information from the mission which you gave me to complete in Sonsonate on the 18th....In that place I interviewed the ringleader Manuel Mojica, one of the most active propagandists of communism....The interview with him convinced me that Bolshevik communism has become second nature to many in that city and other places in the department....In Sonsonate and Izalco...there is much restlessness because of the fear of the communist reaction. They fear pillage and murder, but this is not universal because some of the leading citizens of the said

21. These statements of General Calderón can be found in Méndez, *Sucesos comunistas*, pp. 183-88.

cities say that, as the punishment has been severe, there may not be a revolt, but they allow that the Indians are very tenacious in their ideas.

It is interesting to note the use of the word *Indians* in the last paragraph and also that this same general was in charge of putting down the revolt in January, 1932.

As far as the government and most of the press were concerned, communism was responsible for the outbreaks in the western departments. However, *Opinión Estudiantil,* in its weekly edition of May 23, 1931, presents a different view. Speaking of the inability of the government to handle the worsening situation in Sonsonate, it notes: "The only thing that occurs to these men is repression of a stupid and gross nature against the masses who only hunger and thirst for justice." The paper goes on to note that the government is wrong in attributing the disorders to the communists. They flow, said the writer, from a lack of work, from poor administration and a lack of vision on the part of the government. "If Arturo Araujo wishes to free himself from the specter of communism, he has only to get to work on the organization of his administrative forces." The student newspaper noted that Araujo seemed to fear Martí as if he were the Wandering Jew, suggesting that the communist bugaboo had paralyzed action. Luna and Zapata were not working for the paper at this time and the view given here is that of unhappy but not completely disaffected young Salvadoreans. In their criticisms they appear just, but they overlook the fact that while Martí and company could not have provoked the disorders without the necessary conditions, they had certainly done everything possible to take advantage of them, as the manifesto given above makes clear.

After twenty-six days of hunger strike, Martí was set at liberty on May 31. He left the hospital accompanied by his lawyer, the celebrated jurist Dr. Antonio Pinto Lima. He was met at the hospital gates by a delegation headed by his close friend Doña Adela de Bucaro, who presented him with a glass of orange juice, his first nourishment in almost a month. In a picture posed by Martí and Pinto Lima for *Diario Latino,* he looks thin and very haggard, but he is posturing with a jaunty straw hat and a bow tie as if he had spent the day strolling about town. His supporters immediately carried him in triumph through the streets of the city. Salvadoreans have traditionally loved anyone who can stand up to the petty tyrannies of the state; Agustín Farabundo Martí now became a popular hero among the vast majority of his countrymen, although they were certainly not communist in inclination. May 31, in fact, marks the high point of his career as a successful agitator.

Once released, Martí was taking no chances on immediate rearrest. He disappeared from view. On June 6 *La Prensa* stated that false reports had come in that he was stirring up trouble in Mexico, but really no one knew where he was. The mystery was solved on June 9 when he was captured near Armenia at the *finca* Las Tres Ceibas. He had gone there at the head of some three hundred men to lead a demonstration, but mounted police broke up the meeting and arrested Martí and several others. They were taken to Sonsonate, but not held long. On the thirteenth their release was announced.

The SRI chief then boarded the train for San Salvador, but much to the astonishment of the crowd which awaited him in the capital, he was not on the train when it pulled in. With his typical flair for the dramatic he had disappeared in mid-passage. *Diario Latino* cleared up the mystery on July 4 when it announced: "Martí has not been the victim of foul play and is at liberty." A reporter had gone with him on the train and had seen him hop off at Ateos (a little town down the main line toward San Salvador from Sonsonate). Why this was not reported at the time was not stated.

From that time on there was a notable diminution of the personal appearances of Martí. This does not mean that the extremists were not active. There were still rallies and propaganda, especially during the agitation which began on July 5 with a rally of the Labor party to protest that the party was loyal to Araujo but suspicious of those around him. A student demonstration followed on July 10. Just before, on July 8, *La Prensa* announced that Martí had been seized by the *guardia* at his home in Teotepeque and brought to the capital, where he was being held at the Dirección General de Policía. But he must have been released shortly. It is unfortunate that newspaper censorship after July makes it difficult to follow Martí, but other sources also indicate that he dropped out of sight almost completely. A U.S. naval intelligence report put him at large in San Salvador on July 27.[22]

In September Martí appeared again when a peasant riot at Asuchiyo near the capital brought about a clash between the *campesinos* and the *guardia* in which a dozen men, women, and children were killed. Martí, as leader of SRI, is said to have made a personal visit to Arturo Araujo to protest the action. Araujo detained him for some days. According to Jorge Arias Goméz's biography, at that time the president called Martí before him and offered him a post with the government if he would join the Labor party. Martí refused and soon thereafter was shipped out to Guatemala, but he returned in a few days.[23] This story has also been repeated by other sources with some variations in the details. Martí's protest and arrest seem likely, although the newspapers did not carry any word of such events (they do, however, announce that his right-hand man, Rafael Bondanza, was captured on September 21). But Martí's interview with the president and the offer of a job, some say a ministry, seem unlikely and out of character for the president. Araujo was already deeply in trouble with the conservative classes, the planters, the bankers, and the army, and if Martí were in the government a coup would come almost immediately, as he must have known.

After that Martí went into hiding again. It has been suggested that in October or November he visited Mexico, but it seems more likely that he stayed in the country. Cuenca remembers that Martí spent a good part of those months moving through the western departments, talking to small groups of workers. He never spent more than one or two nights in the same house and was careful not to do anything which would draw

22. N.A., R.G. 59, file 816.00/812.
23. [Arias Gómez], *Martí*, p.19; Luna, "Tragico suceso," p. 60. Serafín Quiteño, among others, believes Martí was offered a government post. I have no doubt that some personal meetings did take place, but the offer of a government position seems highly unlikely.

attention to his presence. When in the capital, he found it necessary to take additional precautions. After the coup of December 2, one of his favorite hiding places in San Salvador was the tomb of former president Manuel Araujo in the General Cemetery, not far from the place where Martí was later executed, and also near the place of his burial. He may have been involved in the outbreak of communist agitation on October 3, in which the *guardia* killed fourteen and wounded fifteen agitators.

The best sources for the activities of his followers during these months are their own manifestos. In one of them, dated August 31, from the Federación Juvenil Comunista, Sect. Salvadoreño, Araujo is accused of "having accelerated the colonization of this country." An apocalyptic vision is presented of a worldwide struggle in which El Salvador will take part, with the workers and the Soviet Union ranged on one side and the capitalists and Yankee imperialists on the other. The workers of El Salvador are urged to "struggle on behalf of the Soviet Union." However, no direct or immediate action is called for.[24]

A captured document of a month later shows the radicals trying to pull their forces together. On October 2, 1931, Ismael Hernández, who had been arrested the previous November with Martí and was a close collaborator with him, issued a manifesto to the SRI locals, signing himself "Secretary General of the SRI." He stressed the following points: (1) All the affiliates of the SRI and their sympathizers ought to be ready to obey all orders coming from the Central Committee of the Communist party and to obey them promptly, without hesitation. (2) No one was to remain inactive in the struggle. (3) But no one was to act without orders from the Central Committee of the Communist party, which, from that moment on, assumed the direction of the movement and placed itself at the head of all revolutionary organizations. (4) The Departmental Executive Committees (of SRI) ought to join themselves through their secretaries-general with the local committees of the Communist party. (6) Strict revolutionary obedience ought to be maintained. A document

24. Osmín Aquirre collection.

issued a few days later by Hernández put one Abel Castro in charge of propaganda for the movement.[25]

Assuming the authenticity of this document, it is by no means certain that it marked the beginnings of preparation for armed revolt. Mario Zapata is supposed to have confided after his arrest: "It is absurd to accuse us of having attempted to implant our reforms by blood and fire,...given the international situation in which we live and the smallness of our territory."[26] Armed revolt was, therefore, only planned when there was no alternative, a situation which came about only after the coup of December 2.

The initial mood of the extreme left was one of cautious optimism about the new government of Hernández Martínez. The first number of *Estrella Roja*, dated December 12, 1931, carried an open letter to the military rulers:

> First of all, let us congratulate you on your *golpe de Estado*. In reality, the blunders of Araujo imposed on the military the moral obligation of overthrowing him, and as these blunders brought us to the point where the country was converted into the prey of his followers, then we agree that your act was heroic and necessary, but, and you must forgive the skepticism, I do not believe that you can solve the Salvadorean crisis which is indescribably more transcendent a problem than your government can handle, the national crisis having roots more profound than the simple incapacity of Don Arturo; it is the inevitable result of the fact that there exists among us a capitalist class which, master of the earth and all means of production, has dedicated itself to a monoculture: coffee, whose ease of exploitation and abundance is obvious.

The next issue of the student publication, December 19, was full of veiled threats to the native aristocracy. Speaking of the

25. Jorge Schlesinger, *Revolución comunista*, pp. 220-21.
26. Buezo, *Sangre de hermanos*, p. 58.

necessity of expropriating the holdings of the landed capitalists, an editorial stated: "One should not refuse a generous indemnity to a capitalist class which, resigned to the inevitable, makes its own Night of August 4 and abolishes its own privileges. On the other hand, the revolution has little inclination to generosity if it encounters resistance."

The same paper also contained an article which seemed to show trust in the new military regime. It spoke again of the government of Arturo Araujo, "overthrown by the generous, legitimate movement of the military youth," and declared "Araujo fell in the midst of general rejoicing. Not a single sector of the populace deplored his downfall....But the situation of the new government is very difficult because economic resources are few and a lamentable disorder reigns. Upon General H. Martínez weighs an enormous responsibility." This surprising moderation might simply have been part of a plot to lull the new government into a feeling of security, but it seems more likely that the idealistic young men who ran *Estrella Roja* were quite sincere in their hopes that reform might make revolt unnecessary. As Martí was to point out, Luna and Zapata were not committed communists who believed that the class struggle must lead to revolution, but visionaries who hoped that somehow El Salvador might be led to a better life.[27] However, these young men were soon to find that their faith in Martínez was badly misplaced. They began to see, especially in the elections of January, 1932, that they could not come to power by any legal means, and that, in fact, General Martínez was preparing their destruction.

From this account of events one might get the impression that communist agitation was all that was going on in El Salvador in 1931. Such an impression would be quite false. Actually, even before the censorship of the press, comparatively few stories were carried which dealt with Martí or his

27. According to Robert Elam, a letter from Martí to Antonio Gil of Puerto Cortez expresses the view that Martínez's takeover made the possibility of a socialist government greater, because nonrecognition would lead to chaos (Robert Varney Elam, "Appeal to Arms: The Army and Politics in El Salvador, 1931-1964" [Ph.D. diss., University of New Mexico, 1968], p. 35).

movement. The average Salvadorean was concerned with a number of other matters, some trivial, some important. There was, for instance, widespread agitation in the press against Chinese merchants, who had been going into the *pupusería* business (the making of tortillas filled with meat, or cheese which are sold in El Salvador like hot dogs in the United States). These foreigners were undercutting local venders and there were demands for their expulsion from the country on the grounds that they were dirty and crooked. The "Yellow Peril" commanded much more attention than the "Red Peril."

In November the center of attention was not Alfonso Luna, but Antonio Luna, "the human vampire," who was being brought to trial for a series of senseless and compulsive murders. In general, the average man was occupied, in that year of depression, with the simple problem of staying alive. That the "popular university" was stirring up trouble out in Sonsonate Department among the despised Indios and poor *campesinos* was common knowledge; that the outcome of this indoctrination might be the most catastrophic incident in the history of the country was something which few even dreamed of.

Chapter 6

The Communist Revolt Begins

Just after the Martínez coup, Major A. R. Harris, who had replaced Col. Cruse as the U.S. attaché for Central American military affairs, paid a visit to El Salvador. His comments are revealing.

About the first thing one observes when he goes to San Salvador is the number of expensive automobiles on the streets. There seems to be nothing but Packards and Pierce Arrows about. There appears to be nothing between these high priced cars and the ox cart with its bare-footed attendant. There is practically no middle class between the very rich and the very poor.

From the people with whom I talked I learned that roughly ninety percent of the wealth of the country is held by about one half of one percent of the population. Thirty or forty families own nearly everything in the country. They live in almost regal splendor with many attendants, send their children to Europe or the United States to be educated, and spend money lavishly (on themselves). The rest of the population has practically nothing....

I imagine the situation in El Salvador today is very much like France was before its revolution, Russia before its revolution and Mexico before its revolution. The situation is ripe for communism and the communists seem to have found that out. On the first of December, 1931, there was in the Post Office in San Salvador over 3,000 pounds of communist literature emanating from New York City, which had been confiscated by the postal authorities during the previous month.

The authorities seem to realize that the situation is dangerous and are quite alert in their fight against communistic influences. One thing in their favor is that the people never go hungry. The poor can always get fruit and vegetables for nothing and they can steal [fire] wood....Also, since they never had anything, they do not feel the want very acutely of things they have never had....A socialistic or communistic revolution in El Salvador may be delayed for several years, ten or even twenty, but when it comes it will be a bloody one.[1]

These are the comments of a shrewd and observant man who saw the revolt coming, though he could not guess how soon his predictions of bloodshed would be fulfilled. His comments illuminate not only the basic causes of the revolt, but also the reasons for its failure, the chief of which was the apathy of the masses to propaganda.

Indeed, the basic causes of the revolt are much clearer than the exact reasons why the revolt occurred when it did. The underlying causes include the deep antagonism between the *campesinos* and the landed gentry, which was seldom noticed by the rich because of the dissembling attitudes of the peasants. There was also a definite racial problem in the Sonsonate area where Indian and Ladino cultures clashed. No amount of insistence on the basic homogeneity of the Salvadoreño stock can disguise the fact that the Indians felt themselves to be different. Added to these basic social causes were economic ones: the monoculture and its collapse in the great depression. A

1. N.A., R.G. 59, Major A.R. Harris, December 22, 1931, file 816.00/828. A couple of months earlier, Finley, the acting chargé d'affaires in San Salvador, had noted that Miguel Dueñas, "the biggest landholder in El Salvador," paid only $5,000 a year in taxes, whereas he should have paid about ten times that amount (N.A., R.G. 59, September 11, 1931, file 816.00/813).

political cause was the tradition of dictatorship and bad government which had made it difficult for the people of Salvador to conduct a normal political life. These elements were all basic to the revolt of January 22, 1932.

As far as the actual communists, and those in sympathy with communism, were concerned, they acted as agents to bring the discontent to a focus, and they provided the machinery through which this discontent could find expression in revolt. In doing this, Martí and his immediate aids, Rafael Bondanza, Ismael Hernández, and Miguel Mármol, appear to have acted largely on their own with a minimum of direction and aid from the international communist movement. Propaganda by the ton they did receive from New York, and some money in small amounts, but the revolt was essentially home-grown. Russia served chiefly as an inspiration to the revolutionaries.

There is one theory that the revolt was not planned at all by the communists and that it was provoked by the government of General Martínez, who deliberately left no road open to social and political change save that of revolt. This belief is very common among informed persons in El Salvador. I have been told that the communists, seeing what was happening, only placed themselves at the head of the doomed movement.

In the generally excellent book of Abel Cuenca we find the following expression:

> From that moment, [the coup of December second] Hernández Martínez began with incredible gall to prepare the repressive machinery of the state, policía, guardia, army, judges, state of siege, etc. with firm determination to crush in blood and fire the mass campesino movement.
>
> The Communist party, which in El Salvador had been organized recently by a small group of dedicated but ideologically and politically weak men, made superhuman efforts to place itself at the head of the popular movement and to channel the discontent of the masses. But it failed. The insurrection, ably provoked by the government, which

had refused recognition of workers' triumphs in the municipal elections, began on January 22. The insurrection lost all direction and expended itself in widespread, chaotic activities of semiarmed bands of men who were rapidly and bloodily put down by the government.[2]

Mauricio de la Selva sees the general's actions as part of his plan to win recognition for his illegal government from the United States by posing as the champion of anti-communism. According to this version, he went so far as to send the army recruits back to their home villages to spread the word that the acting president wanted reforms, but the rich would not allow them unless a *campesino* demonstration changed their minds. "On the other hand, the Communist party leaders tried to avoid the clamor of the poor for an immediate revolt. Finally, Martí was pressured into ordering a revolt for the night of January 22, thus falling into the trap of Maximiliano Hernández Martínez."[3]

Another possibility, suggested by Dr. Alejandro D. Marroquín, is that the dictator's real fear was a Labor party attack based in Guatemala, coinciding with a mass uprising of the peasants on behalf of Arturo Araujo. "He decided to precipitate the rebellion, blame it on the communists, who were growing strong, and crush it by force." This would prevent Araujo from using the masses to regain power, destroy the communist movement, and win friends abroad.[4] The plot, according to Marroquín, was to permit the municipal elections to be held and to allow communist participation, but at the same time to stir up trouble and to blame it on them. In addition, under fear of communism, Martínez organized as "white guards" the Civic Guard in Santa Ana. Then as a last step he rounded up Martí, Luna, and Zapata and circulated rumors of their immediate execution so that the peasants, "who loved Martí," would rise in revolt.[5]

2. Cuenca, *Democracia cafetalera*, p. 32.
3. De la Selva, "Lucha," p. 212.
4. Marroquín, "Crisis," p. 52.
5. Ibid., p. 60.

These versions give Hernández Martínez credit for an almost diabolical cunning. There is no doubt that he wanted the communists crushed, nor that he feared the *campesinos*. Further, the threat of armed invasion from Guatemala was a very real one. But it is unlikely that the general had time or inclination to sit down and think through an elaborate plan which would simultaneously checkmate all his opponents. There were, after all, many factors over which he had no control. He did not know where Martí was or when he might fall into the hands of the police. He was not sure that a communist-led revolt might not succeed, and probably, like almost everyone else, he vastly exaggerated the strength of the movement.

In actual fact, the events of January, 1932, are strikingly like those of December 2, 1931, which brought Martínez to power. In both cases, the general was clever enough to let events take their course and then to capitalize on the mistakes of others when the chance arose. This technique has often been used by military men, including Napoleon the Great. General Maximiliano Hernández Martínez, a bush-league Napoleon, was simply following the same tradition.

On the other hand, it is clear that Martí was no innocent lamb being led to the slaughter. In point of fact, it was he, not Martínez, who planned the revolt and set the date for it. The time when Martí decided upon the date has been the subject of some controversy. Abel Cuenca believes, as do many others, that the revolt was not planned until after the "farce" of the municipal elections; it was the direct result of the realization that it was now impossible to stave off an armed uprising and that it was better to plan it for a certain date than to let the government set the time. He suggested that the correct date for the planning of the revolt would be January 9 or 10. Cuenca himself received his orders on the eighteenth and believes that they had been put out in the capital about the fifteenth.

Jorge Schlesinger, on the other hand, has a photo in his book of a letter which appears to be written by Martí in mid-December to Antonio Gil in Puerto Cortés, Honduras. In it Martí speaks of the revolt as being planned for between the twentieth and twenty-fifth of the coming month.[6] Schlesinger, however, who was writing a paid vindication of the regime of Hernández Martínez, is not completely trustworthy as a source; the letter itself is misdated "December 16, 1932," or a year too late, when Martí would have been dead some ten months. This is the sort of error a forger, writing in 1932, might make, but it could be a slip of the pen on the part of Martí. Judged on internal evidence, the letter could be genuine.

It is entirely possible that Martí had resolved on revolt as soon as Martínez came to power, but did not sit down to plan with his subordinates until after the municipal elections. Certainly, if the necessity for armed revolt did not occur to him until after the electoral frauds of January 3 to 5, he was unduly naive. It was quite clear from the start that Martínez hoped to make himself dictator and that he would revert to the customary Salvadorean electoral process, fraud at the polls. If Martí, despite the weakness of his position, was not thinking of armed revolt, he should have been.

René Padilla Velasco, Martí's lawyer at his final, pre-execution trial, has made the astute comment, "Martí was playing his last card as a leader." The high point of his popularity had been the day of his release after the famous hunger strike. From that time on, the repressive machinery of the Araujo government had cramped his style. He had failed to convert more than a handful of university students to his cause. Only in the western part of the country had he succeeded in building a mass following among the peasants. Even in that section of El Salvador, the area of Communist party influence did not extend north of the volcano Izalco. The city of Santa Ana had a communist movement, especially among the typographers' union, in which Raúl Vides was the leading figure, but these forces were weak and played no part in the revolt. When the test of strength came, either through lack of support or through a communications failure, there were no revolts east of Ilopango. In other words, more than two-thirds of the country had not been properly indoctrinated. Now that a tough dictator had come to power, there would be no opportunity to remedy these defects

6. Jorge Schlesinger, *Revolución comunista*, p. 222.

in the movement, as Martí should have realized. The decision for armed revolt, whenever it was made, should be seen as a desperate gesture to try to dislodge Hernández Martínez before he became overwhelmingly strong.

When he had been in the back country of Nicaragua with Sandino, Martí had written to a friend, "When one cannot write with the pen one must write with the sword."[7] He was now about to put that aphorism into action.

Before Araujo's regime fell, the municipal elections for *alcaldes* (local mayors of the *municipios*) and members of the town councils had been scheduled for December 15. These were to be followed in a few days by the elections for members of the unicameral legislature. The coup made the scheduled elections impossible, but one of the conditions that Castro Canizales and the other leaders of the December 2 coup had imposed on Hernández Martínez was that he hold the elections as soon as possible. The municipal elections were accordingly re-scheduled for January 3, 4, and 5, with the legislative elections to follow on January 10, 11, and 12. The government promised complete freedom in these elections and invited all parties, including the Communist party of El Salvador, to participate. The move was not entirely without guile. In order to vote, one had to be registered in the books kept by each *municipio*, where one inscribed his name and that of his party. Allowing the Communist party to register presented the government with a list of its adherents. When the time came for rounding up communists, the election registers would serve as a handy guide.

Nevertheless, the communists entered their candidates. *Diario Latino* announced on December 12 that Joaquín Rivas was to be the Communist party's candidate for mayor of San Salvador. Alfonso Luna was in charge of Rivas's campaign. The party formed a National Political Elections Commission which put up candidates in as many other towns as possible.

The conduct of these elections was marked by violence. According to the papers of January 5, violence broke out in the *cantón* of Santa Rita, in the Turín district, on January 4. There

7. [Arias Gómez], *Martí*, p. 10.

some four hundred men invaded *fincas* and attacked the National Guard post at Atiquizaya which was commanded by Sgt. Alberto Mathew. The sergeant was gravely wounded and a trooper killed. *Guardia* from Ahuachapán and Santa Ana were then called to the scene. Restoring order, they killed a number of agitators, including Miguel Angel Zelaya and Indalecio Ramírez, leading Reds of the district.

These elections were hardly marked by scrupulous honesty on the part of the government. It is not unfair to speak of an electoral "comedy," in which the government had predetermined the results.[8] In San Salvador the new *alcalde* was Don Roque Jacinto Bonilla of the Partido Fraternal Progresista, a conservative group which also triumphed in the nearby towns of Santo Tomás, Mejicanos, and Santa Tecla, as in Cojutepeque, Acuhuaca, and Comasagua. Joaquín Rivas, the communist candidate, came in third in San Salvador, according to the official tally. The Communist party claimed victory in Santa Tecla, Sonsonate, and elsewhere, but their victories were not certified. No official report of the results of the elections was issued until several days later.

In several towns in the western part of the country, where the Communist party was considered strong, elections were suspended. This took place in Turín, in Tacuba, where Abel Cuenca would have been the Communist party candidate, in Colón, and in a number of small towns throughout Sonsonate Department. While such developments must have been a disappointment to the Red leaders, it is probable that they were aware by then that their choice lay between bloodshed and capitulation. A note from the central committee of the party, written directly after the municipal elections, told the local party chieftains that the Communist party did not really hope to come to power by legal means, but only fought the elections with "the object of preparing the masses for the struggle."[9]

On the seventh of January, according to a news story in *La Verdad*, the party paper edited by Inocente Rivas Hidalgo, the

8. Luna, "Trágico Suceso," p. 61.
9. Jorge Schlesinger, *Revolución comunista*, p. 138.

police went to the Imprenta Cisneros, where *Estrella Roja* was printed, and showed an order from the police director prohibiting the further publication of the student weekly. "Such a measure," thundered *La Verdad*, "does not have the slightest legal foundation and serves only to confirm the present hypocrisy of the government, which, while pretending to concede liberties, constrains liberty of expression." Clearly, relations between the communists and the government were deteriorating.

Another article in the same issue (January 7, 1932) complained bitterly of the lack of freedom shown in the elections. It compared the new regime with those of Quiñónez Molina and the Meléndez brothers, and declared that there had been no electoral freedom. Speaking of the legislative elections, which were coming up in a few days, the newspaper said, "We have presented a list of candidates, hunting for persons we feel are competent and good for such posts. As men we may be in error, but we have not been motivated by malice, and if the electorate find any persons on our lists whom they do not trust they can skip that name." *La Verdad* went on to state that if the next elections proved as fraudulent as the last, it would be up to the army to assert itself against the de facto government of General Martínez. This last statement, which seems puzzling at first glance, was to be explained by the events of the next few weeks, for the party was convinced that it had a strong following in the barracks of the capital.

Also on January 7, violence broke out again in Ahuachapán, where the workers in the coffee fields were on strike. National Guards were summoned to the area, and at the urging of some *finca* owners who gave them liquor, the *guardia* attacked the *campesinos* in a clash that left two dead and four wounded.

General Hernández Martínez was, at this moment, experiencing a severe governmental crisis. Depression conditions had been getting progressively worse since his takeover. He and his supporters began to realize the bitter truth that it was not simply the incompetence of Araujo, but economic forces over which he had little control, that were the cause of El Salvador's difficulties.

On January 8 the government announced new, emergency financial measures which featured a 30 percent reduction in the salaries of all civil servants (except military salaries) and new taxes to bolster the sagging revenue of the government. At this time civil service wages were not only low but were several months behind. However, since the military had manifested its displeasure through the coup d'etat, it was getting paid regularly.

These decrees did not, of course, solve all the government's pressing financial problems. The same day the measures (actually drafted on the seventh) were announced, the president was forced to suffer through a rough meeting with representatives of the *cafetalera,* led by Francisco Dueñas, the greatest of the coffee barons. These men demanded repeal of Araujo's monetary decrees of October prohibiting the shipment of gold abroad, on the grounds that the bankers were using the tight money situation as an excuse for not making loans to the coffee growers. But Martínez refused.

On the next Sunday, January 10, the elections for the legislature began. The conservative Partido Fraternal Progresista boycotted the elections in the capital department on the grounds of electoral fraud. And in the department of San Salvador early returns, published in *La Prensa* on the eleventh, indicated a possible Communist party victory. However, after that date a mysterious silence about the election returns set in, and on January 21 the *Diario Oficial* certified three noncommunists as the winners in San Salvador Department. Voting, it might be noted, had been extremely light, with only a few hundred votes cast in the capital city.

The Sunday of the elections witnessed renewed conflict in the department of Sonsonate, at Armenia, Juayúa, and San Isidro. On the next Tuesday there was an invasion of *fincas* in Turín and around the town of Ahuachapán, where no less than thirty communists were killed.[10]

The communists were no longer relying on election results. On the ninth, before the election of delegates, the central

10. N.A., R.G. 59, McCaffery [sic] to Secretary of State, January 20, 1932, file 816.00/834.

committee of the party issued orders for the formation of a Revolutionary Military Committee, which was to have authority over all comrades on pain of "the most severe discipline." The instructions also set a provisional date for the uprising, January 22. The Revolutionary Military Committee was to be the general staff of the revolutionary army and coordinate its activities. Within the barracks, subversive soldiers were named to take charge of the troops in a mutiny which would be timed to begin with the revolt. A further document, dated January 18, named Inocente Rivas Hidalgo the "Red Commandant" of the Red Army in the San Salvador zone, which, needless to say was critical for the success of the revolt.[11]

One last effort to secure success without revolt was made. The Central Executive Committee appointed a commission consisting of Clemente Abel Estrada, Alfonso Luna, Mario Zapata, Rubén Darío Fernández, and Joaquín Rivas to go to the presidential palace and see if some accommodation could not be worked out. Refused admission to see the president, they talked with his personal secretary, Jacinto Castellanos Rivas, who then arranged a meeting with the minister of war, Col. Joaquín Valdés. The group offered to halt illegal activities and confine the movement to peaceful protest if the government would make substantial contributions to the welfare of the peasants. Otherwise, they warned, there would be a revolt.

According to an observer, Luna told the war minister, "The peasants will win with their machetes the rights you are denying them." To that the latter replied, "You have machetes; we have machine guns." There was no compromise, partly because the delegation admitted that they did not have full authority to call off the projected revolt. By this time, so unsecret had the plans of the conspirators become that the government probably knew the exact moment for which the revolt was planned.

Some leaders were optimistic about the outcome of the proposed revolt. Ismael Hernández, the secretary-general of the SRI, said in a letter that he felt that the U.S., which had not yet

11. Jorge Schlesinger, *Revolución comunista*, pp. 157-58; Alexander, *Communism*, p. 368; Pineda, "Tragedia comunista," *Diario de Hoy*, January 18, 1967.

recognized the new government, would look favorably on the revolt, mistaking it for an *Araujista* counterrevolution, and therefore as an attempt to restore legitimate government. But a letter from Miguel Angel González, evidently written shortly before the insurrection, to the central committee of the Communist party asked realistically if the communist chiefs were sure they had thought out their plan. What were to be the points of concentration? he asked. Who would lead the army? He suggested that they had given little thought to these questions. They believed that a series of uncoordinated attacks, launched at various points from the Guatemalan border to the capital, would be sufficient to topple a military regime having thousands of troops at its disposal, plus the *policía* and *guardia*, and backed by all the resources of the country.[12]

Before the revolution could get off the ground it was dealt three crushing blows. The first of these was the capture of Juan Pablo Wainwright by Ubico in Guatemala, which was announced in the press on Friday, January 15. It meant that the hoped for linkup with forces in Guatemala could not materialize.

Nevertheless, the rebels went ahead with their plans. Schlesinger quotes what he claims were the orders which Martí himself sent out on the sixteenth:

> 2. On January 22 at 12 midnight, all contingents of our revolutionary organization ought to be mobilized and ready for the assault on the barracks of the chief towns in each department and action should commence at once against barracks and posts of police and National Guards....
>
> 4. The revolutionary action against the bourgeoisie ought to be as forceful as possible, in order that in a few hours of merciless terror they will be reduced to the most complete impotence. USE AGAINST THEM THE MOST OPPORTUNE MEANS, THAT IS TO SAY SHOOT IMMEDIATELY OR KILL

12. Jorge Schlesinger, *Revolución comunista*, pp. 121-22, 160.

THEM IN SOME OTHER WAY WITHOUT
DELAY.
    5. ...DO AWAY WITH ALL OF THEM,
SAVING ONLY THE LIVES OF CHILDREN.

If this document is authentic, and I believe that it is, it puts
considerable blame for the frightfulness of the repression on
the fears that the revolt engendered. In actual fact, there was no
"massacre" of the bourgeoisie, but such documents, made public
after the revolt, helped to convince even moderates that the
repression should be severe.

Schlesinger also gives us what appear to be the final orders
for the revolt, prepared around the eighteenth and issued on the
nineteenth. They read as follows:

> From the Central Committee of the Communist
> Party of El Salvador.
>   1. All materials should be issued to the soldiers
> and the manifesto of the Central Committee ought to
> be distributed on midnight of the signaled date....
>   4. The names of the Red Commandants ought to
> be given out at nine on the evening before the
> revolt....
>   7. At 10 P.M., those with that duty ought to
> proceed with the destruction of the rail lines on
> either side of the city and also of the telegraph.[13]

But even as these instructions were going out, two more
crushing blows were dealt the rebels. The first was that Martí
himself was captured; the second, that the plan for the revolt in
the barracks was discovered.

Considerable confusion surrounds the capture of Agustín
Farabundo Martí. Word of his arrest was not made public until
January 20, when it appeared in Diario Latino, which came out
around noon. La Prensa made no mention of the event in the
issue published that morning, but covered the story in detail on
the next day, Thursday, January 21, 1932. This, and the reference

13. Ibid., pp. 171-75.

in *Diario Latino* to Martí's having been taken "last night," has made most writers assume that Martí was captured on the nineteenth. But that date is incorrect: according to Osmín Aguirre y Salinas, Martínez's tough, able chief of police who directed the operation, the capture took place on the evening of January 18.

Confusion also exists concerning the nature of the information leading to the arrest. A commonly believed legend is that the information came from Guatemalan sources after Ubico's capture of Wainwright. Supposedly, one of the latter's men, either because he was a government informer or because he was tortured, told the authorities where Martí might be caught and the information was relayed to San Salvador.

But Martí never stayed anywhere more than a night or two and it is hard to see how anyone in Guatemala would have known where he would be on the eighteenth. Further, Col. Aguirre has assured me that it was a paid informer in the capital who gave him the information that led to the arrest. This man, one of many, was paid about five colones for the information that led to the capture. The informant came to the *policía* early on the afternoon of the eighteenth and told them that Martí would attend a meeting that night in the suburban area of San Miguelito, just north of the city proper on the main road to Mejicanos.

Aguirre dispatched Capt. José Sánchez Angona with ten men to the location named by the informant. This was a small *finca*, rather rundown, located west of the Colegio María Auxiliadora on the site of what is today the church of María Auxiliadora, whose spire dominates the north end of the capital. The *finca* belonged to the Trabanino family, but they were not implicated. Instead there were caretakers, a man and his wife, living in the little house, and they had been persuaded to let Martí use their residence without knowing who he was. At 10:00 P.M. the National Police closed in. With Martí, who surrendered without a struggle, they found Alfonso Luna and Mario Zapata, plus three *campesinos* involved in the movement, and a large quantity of bombs, weapons, and propaganda leaflets in one room.

Martí boastfully told the police that there were more bombs scattered through the city, and according to *Diario Latino* of February 2, thirty-three had been discovered to that date. The capture of the leader also gave the police detailed instructions on the revolt. They allowed the newspapers to publicize on January 21 the fact that an uprising was scheduled for the twenty-second, which presumably they would not have done if they had wanted the communists to go through with the plot, as is often alleged. Martí was taken to police headquarters that night, where he was interrogated. He was brought to the Central Penitentiary at 11:00 A.M. the next morning, according to the prison receipt.[14]

If Martínez had been masterminding the communist plot he could not have done any better for himself. And to top off this unexpected piece of good luck, the only really dangerous part of the revolt, that which was to take place in the barracks of the capital, was a complete failure.

In the barracks of the sixth regiment, which was then being used by the machine gunners (the sixth being at Ahuachapán), on the night of January 16, a soldier named Gonzales presented himself before Sgt. Fernando Hernández. He told the sergeant of a conversation which he had overheard between a pair of corporals named Trejo and Merlos and of a conversation between the corporals and a Sgt. Pérez. These men, according to the informant, were making plans to seize the barracks and capture the officers and noncommissioned officers. Hearing this, Hernández, who was loyal to the regime, approached Sgt. Pérez and pretended to wish to join the conspiracy. Pérez told him that all was ready and that they only awaited the signal for the attack. Hernández got the details of the plot without tipping his hand, and then informed the chief officer of the barracks, who got word to the higher authorities. A secret conference was called by the regimental commander. Here loyal officers and NCOs pooled their information and discovered the fact that the signal for the revolt was to be the approach of an automobile which would toot its horn as a call to seize the officers.

14. Osmín Aguirre collection.

The commandant ordered all officers to remain in the barracks, and confiscated the machine guns of the unit so that they should not fall into the hands of the mutineers. This move caused a stir among the troops and a brief, premature uprising on January 18. Upon being questioned, the soldiers who were involved implicated Joaquín Rivas and one Carlos Hernández as their links with the communists in the city, and further stated that Alfonso Luna and Mario Zapata were part of the conspiracy.

The same night, the eighteenth, witnessed a serious disturbance in Barrio de Concepción, where a crowd of about five hundred "attacked police bringing in a prisoner." This could have been a halfhearted attempt to rescue Martí, as the crowd was said to have been shouting communist slogans, and the communist leader might have been conveyed through that district on his way to the police station.

At any rate, the officers of the machine gun regiment were now alerted. On the evening of the next day, they trained their machine guns to rake the area around the *cuartel*, and waited. A car with lights out approached, stopped before the gate, and honked. It was immediately received with a hail of bullets— then it started up, sheered around, and tore off down the street.

In the famous First Cavalry Regiment Barracks, which lies northeast of the city (and is now the Policía de Hacienda), signs of unrest had also been noted. The soldiers began to behave oddly, making vague references to some kind of catastrophe and refusing to look the officers in the eye. This seriously alarmed the *oficiales* who, like their counterparts in the machine gunners, held a council of war and decided to confiscate all the automatic weapons and distribute them among the officers. At night the officers stationed themselves in a manner so that they could sweep the barracks with fire to resist an outside attack. Here too, the expected violence came on the night of the nineteenth, about 10:30 P.M.

The officers of the First Cavalry began to notice unusual activity outside the barracks. Groups of men were collecting some distance from the barracks, which lay in the countryside at that time. After a while they moved forward and it could be seen that they were armed with pistols, a few rifles, and, of course, the ubiquitous machete. The sentry at the gate challenged them nervously; when they failed to halt, he raised his piece and fired a wild shot over their heads. The attackers at once opened fire, as did the hidden officers behind the high, crenellated walls of the barracks. The attackers fell back into the hills and gullies which surrounded the fort.[15]

Describing the attack two days later, *Diario Latino* claimed that the machine guns had blazed away for an hour at the hidden attackers and that at the end of that time there were more than fifty attackers killed and many more wounded. It is doubtful that this number was ascertained by body count; it would be highly unlikely for men firing machine guns at night to total up so high a figure. In this war, as in all others, casualty estimates must be taken with a grain of salt.

The reason why the attacks at the barracks took place on the nineteenth rather than on the scheduled date of the revolt is difficult to discover, but Martí's arrest the night before probably had something to do with it. Also, by that date, the leaders outside the barracks knew that their plans had been discovered by the officers of the various regiments. All the same, it was tactically stupid to push up the date of this attack. If the uprising in San Salvador had taken place on schedule it would have prevented the government from sending troops to the west and might have prolonged the revolt, though it is doubtful if Julius Caesar himself could have saved the cause at that point.

Another effect of the premature revolt was to give the government ample cause to proclaim a state of siege. Carried in the papers on January 21, the proclamation announced that a state of siege was in effect for the six western departments of Ahuachapán, Sonsonate, Santa Ana, La Libertad, San Salvador, and Chalatenango. Martial law was proclaimed for the entire country. Pointing to the pamphlets and explosives captured with

15. The material on the attack on the barracks was compiled from a variety of sources: [Arias Gómez], *Martí*, p. 23; Joaquín Castro Canizales [Quino Caso], "Acontacimientos de enero de 1932," *Tribuna Libre*, January 19 and 21, 1952; *La Prensa*, and *Diario Latino*, January 19, 20, and 21, 1932.

Martí as well as to the barracks assaults, the government justified its actions to the people: "As a result, the supreme government, conscious of its duty to watch over the peace and constitutional principles [this from Hernández Martínez!] and to maintain the national laws, finds itself obligated to decree drastic measures."

A further decree instituted rigorous press censorship, demanding that all articles in newspapers be submitted to the chief of police before publication. Poor El Salvador! lamented *Diario Latino*. "It seems that El Salvador is condemned to live perpetually under a regime of force, at least so we judge the meaning of the state of siege. We have scarcely succeeded in suspending the emergency decrees caused by the overthrow of Araujo by the army." But *Diario Latino* should have saved its laments. The headlines of the next few days would be a good deal grimmer.

Chapter 7
The Revolt in Juayúa and Nahuizalco

All real hope of success was now gone. With the crushing of the movement in the barracks and the capture of Martí, a mass roundup of known radicals began. In desperation, the Communist party leaders met on the night of the twentieth. Some argued that the only way to salvage the situation was to begin the revolt at once. Others pointed out the impossibility of success. Their arguments against senseless bloodshed were valid, but their opponents were able to counter that if they did not go through with the plan the masses would consider them traitors and cowards.[1] In the end, a halfhearted attempt was made to call off the revolt. Instructions were sent out on January 21, but most of them miscarried—at least those going to the critical western region. Government vigilance had made communications very difficult.

Between January 19 and 21 a number of alarming reports had begun to filter into the capital. The government, having proclaimed a state of siege, made various dispositions for defense, regrouping and consolidating the *guardia*; but these efforts, like those of the enemy to call off the revolt, seem to have been halfhearted. The country moved like a sleepwalker toward disaster.

The revolt came on the very night for which it was predicted, the night of January 22/23 (not the previous night, as some have erroneously believed). One of the most fierce assaults, and the most successful, was made on the town of Juayúa, which lies some thirteen miles north of Sonsonate just off the road to Ahuachapán, in a valley between the volcano Izalco and the

1. [Arias Gómez], *Martí*, p. 23.

mountain Apaneca. It was a coffee town with a population of two or three thousand, surrounded by *fincas* and *beneficios*.

Today Juayúa is perhaps the most pleasant little village in El Salvador. The streets are clean and paved. The town square has a beautifully maintained garden filled with lush tropical flowers. The only unsightly element on the square is an elaborate border of painted signs surrounding the little park, advertising the ruling party in the *municipio*, the Christian Democratic Party (PDC). The people here seem better fed and better dressed than elsewhere, the girls, wandering down the streets on a sleepy Sunday afternoon, handsomer than girls elsewhere in the republic—and dressed in well-filled slacks too, which is unusual in conservative El Salvador.

In those days, however, the town was sunk in abject poverty because of the collapse of coffee prices. Ever since August, 1931, there had been rumors of impending doom. The communists, despite the efforts of the municipal authorities, had been growing strong in the *cantones* around the town. The leading figure in the radical movement was Francisco, or Chico, Sánchez, a short, rough little Indian who was the unofficial cacique of the Indian community who lived mostly back in the *cantones* scattered through the surrounding hills. Although a poor farmer himself, Sánchez had a vast ascendency among his race, and when he was convinced to join the revolutionary movement, he brought the whole community with him. Sánchez had two grown sons, Felipe and Napoleon, who were also active in the movement. In addition to the Sánchez family, other leaders of the revolt included Lucas Zavalete and Benjamín Herrera; the latter is generally regarded as the man most responsible for the atrocities which took place.

The government had long been suspicious of Chico Sánchez's activities, and he had been arrested just after the coup of December 2 and taken to the capital. He was released and returned to Juayúa, only to be arrested again on January 3, the day of the municipal elections, probably for some kind of election protest. He was let go that same evening in San Salvador, and set off for home with a man described as "a communist agent." After stopping at Nahuizalco and conferring with other leaders, Chico Sánchez returned to Juayúa to make more mischief.[2]

When the reporter, Joaquín Méndez, Jr., visited the town of Juayúa a few days after the uprising, he was shown a number of documents captured from the rebels. The first was a list of persons contributing money to the revolutionary cause. It ran to 484 names, which gives some idea of the strength of the movement in that area and of Sánchez personally. In another document, Méndez noted, Chico Sánchez was appointed financial secretary of the local chapter of FRTS. He saw a number of other papers relating to SRI and the Communist party, indicating that the conspirators had been very busy indeed in Juayúa.

Despite the fact that the authorities were aware of this, and since the twenty-first had been aware of an impending attack and a state of siege, the actual attack seems to have taken everyone by surprise. In view of the possibility of an armed revolt the National Guard had been regrouped, and there were no troopers in Juayúa when the blow fell. The only armed force consisted of two local policemen. On the twenty second, the city fathers called Sonsonate to ask for reinforcements; that duty done, they went cheerfully off to bed without taking any special precautions.

Some persons had even had a private warning. The most respected man in town was an Italian immigrant, Don Emilio Redaelli. He was the manager of the *beneficio* of the Daglio family, who were among the wealthiest of the coffee growers. Dr. Máximo Jérez, himself a leading citizen of the town, told Méndez after the revolt that Redaelli was "a great man. Although he was a foreigner, he was a Salvadorean as much or more than anyone else. There was not a good work in which he did not take part. On occasions he had aided economically the municipal government and the schools. All the progressive works in the area were due to him. He was the man of Juayúa." This was certainly true. Word of his charities had frequently appeared in the press of the capital; only a couple of months earlier, on November 12, *La Prensa* noted that Redaelli had

2. Méndez, *Sucesos comunistas*, p. 79.

distributed fifty colones among the successful students of Juayúa after their final exams. He was the outgoing *alcalde* of the town.

Redaelli received a visit from one Concepción Molina who had been a Communist party candidate in the recent elections. Molina told Redaelli that there was certain to be an attack on the town, but that he need not worry, for neither he nor others would be harmed.[3] The warning was all too correct, but the promise turned out to be false.

The town of Juayúa went peacefully to bed at ten o'clock. Izalco, in eruption, was only a few miles away, and though it was a moonlit night, the moonlight had to filter through a haze of ashes. At about eleven the more restless sleepers might have heard voices in the darkness as groups of men began to assemble. These men, some five hundred of them under the leadership of the Sánchez family and Benjamín Herrera, were armed with machetes, knives, clubs, and a surprising number of rifles. (The last were the unintentional gift of Don Arturo Araujo; he had planned to make a stand in the neighborhood when he was fighting to retain power before he slipped across the border into Guatemala, and had therefore stockpiled rifles.) At 11:50 P.M. on the night of the twenty second, the rebels launched their attack by storming the telegraph office. The office was located about five hundred yards from the house of the *alcalde*, who was awakened from his sleep by the sound of machete blows against the doors of the station. The telegraph operator, Felipe Herrera, and his son Teodoro Herrera escaped by jumping through a window. The communist-led rebels later conducted a search for them, but were unable to find them. The Herreras were lucky; telegraph operators were among the principle victims of the uprising, along with local commandants and *alcaldes*. The reason was, of course, that only the telegraph wires connected these towns with the outside world and it was necessary to seal off communications. Then too, the operators were identified with "the establishment" in the eyes of the peasants. At least one operator met death by torture.[4]

3. Ibid., pp. 57-58, 68-69, 79.
4. *La Prensa*, January 27, 1932.

After sacking the office and destroying the equipment of the station, the rebels set off for the *cabildo*. The town's two police officers, Octavio Pérez and Abel Asencio, were staying there. The mob broke down the door using machetes and clubs and attacked the two men inside. Pérez, who tried to resist, was captured and brutally murdered after first having his hands cut off because he had resisted. Abel Asencio managed to flee to a nearby house and find shelter there.[5]

By now the whole of Juayúa was awake and the confusion must have been horrific. According to an eyewitness, "All ran to the darkest corners of their houses, in order not to be victims of the Reds, others put on red insignia, repugnantly, to save themselves." The *indígenas rojas*, as this witness ambiguously called them, broke into stores and opened cases of wine and beer. Showing traditional Salvadorean passion, they set off fireworks to celebrate their victory,[6] and the sound must have reached the ears of the terrified townspeople as firing squads rather than fireworks. The sacking of the shops, which became the major goal of the rebels in each town, was due not only to a natural desire for food, liquor, and clothing, but also to the traditional hostility between the *campesinos* of the outlying *cantones* and the town merchants who they felt defrauded them.

When the invaders had made sure of the *cabildo*, the better organized among them set off for the house of Don Emilio Redaelli, the Italian philanthropist. It was a solid, masonry structure with a massive door of wood reinforced with iron. Against this stout door the rebels banged for some time. Don Emilio himself, a round-faced, surprisingly northern looking man with steel-rimmed glasses and an owlish expression, then appeared on the balcony, overlooking the street, with a pistol in his hand. "What do you want?" he called.

"Some money," someone answered, but as he turned to go, presumably to get some money, they began to cry, "No, no, the life of the rich, the *patrones*." Then Redaelli appeared on the balcony again with his wife and son clutching him. The crowd began to stone him. Don Emilio was struck down and wounded

5. Méndez, *Sucesos comunistas*, p. 80.
6. Alfredo Schlesinger, *La verdad*, pp. 92-95.

by a stone, a bullet, or some other missile. His door finally gave way under repeated blows and the rebels swarmed in. After breaking into Redaelli's house, according to Jorge Schlesinger, the peasants violated his wife in his presence and then dragged the wounded man out of the house. They tied him by his thumbs and dragged him about the town, submitting him to a number of tortures. After several hours of this the battered Redaelli asked for water and, according to Col. Julio Calderón, *"Los bandidos le orinaban la boca."* His agony did not end until the next day, January 23, around three in the afternoon. The fatal blow was struck by Benjamín Herrera.[7]

Redaelli's frightful murder became a symbol of the revolt, and helped to unite most Salvadoreans against the rebels. Why he was selected for such brutal treatment remains a mystery. It is possible that his philanthropic reputation was a mere front, or that Sánchez or Herrera had something against him personally. More likely, he was victimized because he was identified in the minds of the peasants with the Daglio family.

Another murder was that of the local commandant. The commandants, usually retired army officers, are local officials charged with the military preparedness of the area and recruiting (that is, rounding up by force) draftees for the army. In Juayúa the commandant was Col. Mateo H. Vaquero, who lived about two hundred yards south of the town hall. According to an often quoted story, Vaquero was being dragged from his house by the rebels when his three-year-old daughter ran up and threw herself over his body, but failed to stop the machete blows which killed the commandant and cut off her leg.[8]

A number of other atrocities are said to have been committed. Gustavo Pineda tells of a lady, whose name (for obvious reasons) he does not mention, who was dragged off into the bushes and raped by a number of the rebels. "By some

7. Ibid.; Jorge Schlesinger, *Revolución comunista*, pp. 192-93; Méndez, *Sucesos comunistas*, pp. 82-83; Col. Julio C. Calderón, "Memorial histórico: Lo que no se dijo de la rebelión comunista en Ahuachapán, Sonsonate y Santa Ana en el año 1932" (Unpublished manuscript in the hands of Miguel Pinto, Jr.), p. 3.
8. Julio Calderón, "Memorial histórico," pp. 3-4; Alfredo Schlesinger, *La verdad*, p. 95.

miracle they left her with her life. Returning to her home, she felt one day the effects of the outrage. Very indignant, she thought for a moment of an abortion, but as a sincere Catholic consulted her confessor. 'As a religious person you should not do that. God will inspire you to endure.' And a girl child was born."[9]

It is also said that a townsman named Margarito Soriano was murdered sometime during the uprising when he failed to give enthusiastic enough *vivas* for Socorro Rojo. And Col. Calderón, who was there not long after the revolt, reports that Chico Sánchez personally set an example of barbarism "by violating two sisters, aged eleven and thirteen, daughters of a distinguished family of the town."[10] There were also many instances of arson: Redaelli's house was set afire with gasoline, and a number of stores were burned after being sacked, among them that of another foreigner, Leopoldo Chong, a Chinese.

Not all the houses of the rich were put to the torch, however. Dr. Jérez noted to the reporter Joaquín Méndez, Jr., that his house was not burned although it was near the telegraph office which was destroyed by fire. The doctor said it was spared because the leaders of the movement planned to take over the best houses for themselves. "I heard perfectly...when one of them said to his companion, 'No, no, not this one, this is for the chief.'"[11]

Chico Sánchez, who must have been a flamboyant little villain, expressed his whimsy by commanding the town band to appear daily in the plaza and serenade the rebels. Whenever he got the urge, he would command, "Let the band play," and play away they would for dear life until he commanded them to stop. Unlimited power appears to have released his musical as well as his baser passions. But to further humiliate the wealthy, the women of the best families were requisitioned to grind corn (normally a task left to their maids) for the rebel · forces. Perhaps they were subjected to jibes and molestations, but the recollection of most is that there were few, if any, cases

9. Pineda, "Tragedia comunista," *Diario de Hoy*, January 20, 1967.
10. Julio Calderón, "Memorial histórico," p. 4.
11. Méndez, *Sucescos comunistas*, p. 61.

of rape other than those mentioned above.[12] On the other hand, both reporters and eye-witnesses claim that the rebels were planning a *noche de bodas* in which they planned to seize all the pretty young girls of the town on the evening of the twenty-fifth and parcel them out among the revolutionary forces. Other sources label the idea as the hysterical imaginings of the town women, who, God knows, had reason enough to be hysterical; I am inclined to agree that anything so formal as this projected *noche de bodas* seems out of character with the rest of the revolt.[13] Whatever the truth regarding that particular plot, the realities of Indian occupation must have been bad enough for the middle-class Ladino citizens of Juayúa.

Here, as in other more remote locations, the rebels assumed for the first day or so that the uprising had been universally successful and that they were in complete control of the country. Their first taste of disillusionment came on the second day of the revolt, when an airplane appeared at 6:30 A.M. and circled the town. Thinking that it was a friendly plane, the mob ran into the street, shouting and waving. Thereupon the airplane calmly dropped a bomb into their midst. The bomb did no particular damage, but it rudely awakened the rebels to the facts of life. They began to make plans for the defense of Juayúa.

The rebels had also seized the little hamlet of Salcoatitán, which lay two miles from Juayúa on the road down to Sonsonate. As in Juayúa, they attacked on the night of January 22, about midnight. The *cabildo*, telegraph station, and *guardia* station were burned, and of course, the main business of sacking the town was well attended to.

These events in Juayúa and Salcoatitán were soon reported in Nahuizalco, some six miles south of the latter in the direction of Sonsonate. The town was connected to Juayúa not only by the main road, but by a secondary road which ran parallel to it about two miles to the east and snaked around Salcoatitán.

12. In fact, a letter from a citizen of Juayúa, printed in *La Prensa*, February 7, 1932, denies that there were *any* rapes and also denies the story that women of quality were put to grinding corn.
13. For this story recounted as true see Jorge Schlesinger, *Revolución comunista*, pp. 193-94; Méndez, *Sucesos comunistas*, pp. 60-61, 103. The story is denied by Buezo, *Sangre de Hermanos*, p. 72.

Nahuizalco was, therefore, an obvious goal for the rebels in Juayúa.

Today, Nahuizalco presents a remarkable contrast to its neighboring town. If Juayúa is one of the most handsome villages of the region, Nahuizalco is one of the more depressing. The church stands at the end of a bumpy street, and around the church there is no proper square but only a muddy, tramped-down area with trees along the edge and venders' shacks where one can buy *cerveza* and *pupusas*. In those days, there was probably little difference between the towns as far as misery was concerned.

On hearing of the seizure of Juayúa, the people of Nahuizalco began to make urgent preparations for departure. Various Ladino families headed off into the hills. By this method some saved themselves, hiding in the ravines until the attack was over; many others were seized by the rebel forces, while some returned to town quickly with the news that the surrounding hills were filled with bands of armed marauders. A landholder, who ran into the mob and lived to tell the tale, recalled: "Being in a hurry to get to Nahuizalco, they contented themselves with threats and assured me I would be among the first to fall into their hands. In the confused mass of the crowd there were about two hundred of my own boys, my neighbors and brothers...whom we had paid with religious punctuality."[14]

If one stands on the very rim of the volcano Izalco and looks beyond the black mass that slopes out from one's feet, the devil's ski run of hardened ash from which the volcano is made, one can see the towns of Nahuizalco, Izalco, and Sonsonate spread out before the eye as clearly as on a map, forming a triangle, the base of which would be a line between the two smaller centers and the apex, farthest away, would be Sonsonate. Beyond Sonsonate one would see the green fruit trees and pasture land stretching away to Acajutla, and so great is the height, and so clear the air in smog-free El Salvador, that today one can make out the ocean-going ships in the open roadstead and the undulating white line of the

14. *La Prensa*, February 4, 1932.

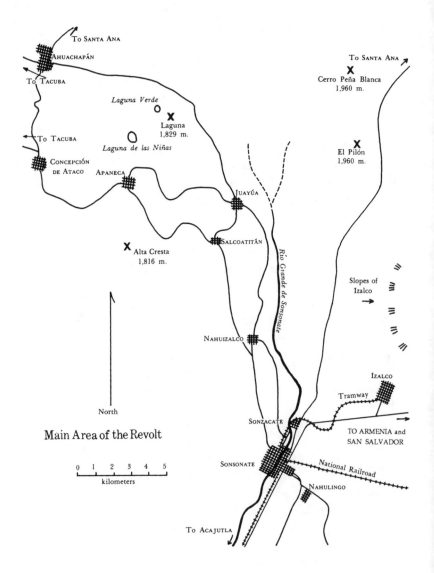

To Santa Ana

Ahuachapán

To Tacuba

To Tacuba

Laguna Verde

Laguna
1,829 m.

Laguna de las Niñas

Concepción
de Ataco

Apaneca

Juayúa

Salcoatitán

Alta Cresta
1,816 m.

To Santa Ana

Cerro Peña Blanca
1,960 m.

El Pilón
1,960 m.

Río Grande de Sonsonate

Slopes of
Izalco

Nahuizalco

Izalco

Tramway

North

Main Area of the Revolt

Sonzacate

TO ARMENIA and
SAN SALVADOR

Sonsonate

National Railroad

0 1 2 3 4 5
kilometers

Nahulingo

To Acajutla

breakers with the deep green sea beyond. On the morning of January 23, 1932, it would have been unwise to stand there, because the volcano was in full eruption; but if one had been able to, he would have seen smoke and flames arising from half a dozen locations, with the largest mass of black smoke rising over the shoulder of the hill that hid Juayúa from view. On the roads, long caterpillars of bobbing white shirts would have marked the movements of angry mobs who were marching away from the *cantones* along the slopes of the volcano region and into Nahuizalco and Izalco, ever closer to Sonsonate itself.

By 9:00 A.M. that morning, the mood in Nahuizalco among the middle-class citizens was pure hysteria. They realized now that all avenues of escape were blocked and they could do nothing to defend themselves. Although the Indian cacique, Felipe Nerio, had been threatening the revolt for months, no one had thought to lay in a supply of arms and ammunition. At that hour, a car drove into town filled with radical leaders, probably including Nerio himself, Communist party boss Tomás Gonzales, and Juan Isidro Pérez. They told the inhabitants that they had them at their mercy and they would return to occupy the town at ten o'clock that evening. They warned the townspeople that if they had failed to make up their minds to join the revolt by that time they must suffer the consequences. Although they realized the gravity of the situation, few citizens among the Ladinos of Nahuizalco were willing to join the movement. More realistic than their opponents, they knew that chances of success were small and reprisal almost certain. "You can imagine what moments of anguish we felt, lacking any means to defend ourselves," said Don Alejandro Ayala in testimony after the revolt. The "Red Army" leaders left and the townsfolk scurried about making what preparations they could, at least hiding their daughters and their valuables in safe places. But, evidently impatient with the refusal of the citizens to join them at once, the revolutionaries anticipated their set hour, returning in force at 3:00 P.M. About five hundred men entered the town, armed with machetes and crying, "Viva Socorro Rojo!" and other communist-inspired slogans. The invaders, mostly Indians but with some Ladinos among them, declared that the country was theirs and resistance was useless.

The rebels set fire to a number of shops, including one belonging to the prosperous merchant Reyes Salavaria, and the pharmacies of Alfredo Alvarado and Ismael Rodríguez. They would have set fire to the church with gasoline, but at the precise moment they were going to enter the building, the church bells began to toll mysteriously and the superstitious mob recoiled in horror.

Outside of looting and arson, events in Nahuizalco were relatively tame. Two citizens of the town, Antonio Martínez and Alejandro García, were killed by the rebels. Antonio Roca lost an arm and sustained fourteen machete wounds, but survived, and a man called Rafael Ramos was also wounded. The commandant, Major Renaga, was not harmed. Nonetheless, Nahuizalco, which has been remodeled less than other towns since that time, shows more traces of the revolt today than can be found anywhere else. Numerous doors can still be seen with deep machete gashes in them, carefully painted over each time the door is repainted. Evidently these doors saved many people from molestation; most of them are about two inches thick, strong enough to withstand the hard blows of the machetes.[15]

Having made themselves masters of three towns north of Sonsonate, and thus effectively cutting communications between that town and Ahuachapán, Chico Sánchez and his fellows had little to do but amuse themselves and wonder how the revolt was going elsewhere. The key to the situation in the western part of the country was the city of Sonsonate itself, and Indians from the Juayúa area, as well as from Izalco, participated in the attack on the city. The conflict at Sonsonate was crucial; but the revolutionaries were also dealing severe blows in other parts of the country.

15. Ibid.; Jorge Schlesinger, *Revolución comunista*, p. 190; Méndez, *Sucesos comunistas*, pp. 36-37; and interviews.

Chapter 8

The Revolt in Other Areas

The town of Colón lies at the foot of a long hill that runs down from Santa Tecla. Today a four-lane highway goes in that direction, often cut out of solid rock—a road so steep that the ramshackle Salvadorean buses puff and heave on the way up, and sometimes don't make it. Between the two towns, the road passes Los Chorros, a series of three semi-natural bathing pools that look like something out of a Tarzan movie and are the pride and joy of the ministry of tourism (most Salvadoreans can't or at least don't swim).

The Communist party had been very active around Colón. During the municipal elections they had put up a slate consisting of José María Iraheta for *alcalde*, Ramón Pacheco and Joaquín Valencia for *regidores*, and Alfredo Godoy for *síndico*. But the elections there had been cancelled, much to their irritation. In the legislative elections they abstained. Everyone feared they would resort to violence. A contingent of National Guards, in town during the legislative elections, had disarmed as many of the local peasants as they could, collecting ninety-six *corvos*, the long, straight, thin-bladed Salvadorean machetes. There were a number of warnings passed for citizens to be on the alert.

Sr. Federico Portillo, a prominent native of the town, decided to take some action against a possible uprising. On the twenty-second he went to the plantation of a Mr. Dalton and borrowed from Dalton a carbine and some ammunition, returning to town that evening with a single friend. As the two men came to the national highway (then a dirt road) from the Dalton hacienda they noticed some hostile-looking and mysterious groups of men moving in the direction of Colón; but as it was now after dark, the two men were not seen by the mob. They crept cautiously along the side of the highway, arriving at the town about three o'clock on the morning of January 23. As they slipped into Colón they saw that the door of the *alcaldía* had been forced open and stood ajar. Portillo, who was armed, decided to investigate. Poking inside with his carbine ready, he tripped over the drawers of cabinets that had been tossed about along with chairs, tables, and the contents of the drawers. As he felt his way across the room he kicked into two bodies: one, the municipal secretary, Efraín Alvarenga, had been hacked to death by machete blows; the other, Damasio Cruz, a local policeman, was still alive but seriously wounded by a gunshot. The rebels who had pillaged the office had taken the confiscated *corvos* and some carbines.[1]

It seemed that the mob had arrived shortly before 2:00 A.M. and had remained in the town about an hour. They had sacked the *alcaldía*, the *comandancia*, and the telegraph office. The telegraph operator, Félix Rivas, survived the attack and gave his story to *Diario Latino* where it was printed on February 1, 1932. He told how he had been violently awakened by the sounds of stones being thrown against his house and the door being battered down with machetes and clubs. No sooner was he out of bed than the door gave way and the rebels fell upon him crying, "Viva el Socorro Rojo," and "Viva la República Soviética." He attempted to resist, but a tremendous blow fell on his shoulders and he lay stunned, unable to move. His wife was likewise cut down but not killed. When rescuers discovered Rivas as they hunted about the town with lanterns after the attack, he had wounds in all parts of his body. His hands had been hacked off and one of his eyes was put out. For several days he was kept under intensive care in a San Salvador hospital and was not expected to live.

The local commandant, taken by surprise in the *comandancia*, had not been so lucky. He was hacked to death by a man later identified to the police by his wife as Antonio Avelar Sosa, who was one of the ringleaders. The attack had

1. Méndez, *Sucesos comunistas*, pp. 156-58.

been planned by Avelar Sosa, Simeón Cerbellón, Brigido Monzón, Andrés Torres, and several others who had been meeting out at the house of Andrés Torres' father, Regino, in Las Moras, a *canton* of Colón.[2]

Another victim was Doctor Jacinto Colocho Bosque of Chalatenango; he had heard that there was trouble around Santa Ana and was on his way to see about the safety of his family, who lived there. With him in his car were his driver, his wife, Doña Soledad, and his close friend Victor Durán, the former *alcalde* of Chalatenango. Passing a place called El Zanjón on the outskirts of Colón as they drove down the national highway from Santa Tecla, they ran into a mob of about three hundred men at 10:30 P.M. on the night of January 22. Many other members of the upper classes had met such groups and had been lucky enough to get off with a few threats; but in this instance, either the men in the car talked back to the mob, or the crowd was in a tougher mood than usual, for they dragged the three men from the car and hacked them to death with *corvos*. The señora was wounded, but managed to escape with her life.[3]

Perhaps that same mob, or one of equal ferocity, came upon a poor *campesino* named Jesús Cruz, a *mozo* of one Sra. Nuila. The man was leading some mules loaded with her merchandise. When he refused to hand over these goods to the mob they killed him. Near the *finca* Las Delicias, closer to the outskirts of Santa Tecla, they met and killed a poor woman who ran a small vending stand. The crowd also ran into Dr. Abraham Chavarría, riding a horse in the area. Wisely, he did not resist and was only robbed of his money, horse, and pistol.[4]

The citizens of Colón, thankful that their unwelcome guests had not remained longer, prepared to defend themselves against any fresh assault. Portillo and the other townsmen gathered together what arms they had and waited. On January 23, about eight in the morning, a group of four hundred men were seen advancing on the town. The citizens of Colon ordered

2. Osmín Aguirre collection. This is from a police document. The commandant was Col. Domingo Campos.
3. *La Prensa*, January 28, 1932. On February 6 the same paper announced the capture of the assassins.
4. *Diario Latino*, January 28, 1932.

them to halt, and the rebels responded by opening fire. As the townsmen returned the rebel fire, the *campesinos* broke and fled. In the peasant ranks one of the first to fall was Isabel Zaldade, seventy-eight years of age, who had been Communist party candidate for *alcalde* of Sacacoyo in the recent elections.[5]

One reason for the ease with which the second attack was repulsed might have been the fact that just before, the rebels had made an unsuccessful attempt to take Santa Tecla, the capital of La Libertad Department. A group, estimated at several thousand by some observers, set out for Santa Tecla, up the long hill, early that morning. Near a *finca* between Colón and Las Delicias which belonged to Sr. Guirola, one of the most prominent Salvadorean landholders, the rebel force ran into a patrol under the command of regular army Captain Salvador Iraheta, who was part of the garrison of the provincial capital. To disperse the mob, Capt. Iraheta ordered his men to fire into the air, but this only brought return shots from the *campesinos*, who rushed toward the badly outnumbered patrol with raised machetes. The troops then fired into them, but the situation was critical: giving away slowly so the mob could not come to hand-to-hand fighting, they fired their antiquated bolt-action Mausers as rapidly as they could, until, at last, a relief force under Colonel Salvador Ochoa arrived. These National Guards, mounted on a truck, had a machine gun with them which they soon brought into play, making havoc in the rebel ranks.[6] In that way the attack on Santa Tecla (or Nueva San Salvador) was broken up. It was probably this same group of badly shaken and decimated rebels that was encountered by Portillo and the solid citizens of Colón. There were no deaths reported among the army, *guardia*, or civilian groups who fought against the *campesinos* in these two actions. Rebel casualties were evidently heavy.

Although Colón and Santa Tecla beat off the attackers, a number of small towns in the department of La Libertad were overrun, including Los Amates, Finca Florida, Teotepeque, and Tepecoyo. Martí's town of Teotepeque was taken over briefly on

5. Méndez, *Sucesos comunistas*, p. 158.
6. Ibid., pp. 175-76.

January 23 by a small group armed only with machetes. They were quickly driven out by a group of *guardia*, according to *La Prensa* on the twenty-sixth. At Jayaque, one of the richest coffee areas of the country, a large mob broke up and ran when a government aircraft swooped low over them. None of these attacks resulted in any more damage than a few shops sacked.

In the port city of La Libertad (El Salvador's chief link with the outside world and the port for San Salvador), the populace were in a state of panic. But the commandant of the town, Lt. Col. Santiago Ayala, organized a civic guard which manned barricades along the three roads leading down into the town. Only once did they spot anything which might have been an attack, and that was dispersed with a few shots.

There was considerable activity just east of San Salvador. The region around Lake Ilopango had been the birthplace of the Communist Party of El Salvador, and the communists were strong in Ilopango and Soyapango, a suburb of San Salvador. On the twenty-ninth, *Diario Latino* spoke of an alarm over an attempt to poison the city water supply in that area, while *La Prensa*, a day earlier, reported that the garrisons of the towns had been attacked, but had driven off the attackers, inflicting heavy losses. Seventeen bodies were left behind by the rebels on that occasion, but evidently no troops were killed. At the little village of Asino, on the lake, bands of disorganized rebels could be seen wandering about after these unsuccessful forays, which evidently took place on the twenty-third. Meanwhile, near Panchimalco, the historic Pipil Indian town with its ghostly colonial church, the rebels stole some cattle and ate them but did no further damage.

Far to the west, in the border region around Ahuachapán, there were serious disturbances. Several *fincas* were burned at Chalchuapa, site of the ancient ruins of Tazumal, on the road between Ahuachapán and Santa Ana. Similar instances of arson apparently occurred at El Congo, south of Santa Ana. There was, however, no serious violence at either place.

But Ahuachapán itself had long been a center of communist-inspired disorders. The "popular university" had attracted thousands of local *campesinos* to come and listen to leftist orators, including home-town boy Alfonso Luna. In the municipal elections of January 3, the communists had put up for the post of *alcalde* one Marcial Contreras, a leading spokesman of the radical left, and had paraded through the city in an imposing display of strength. The very look of those disciplined hordes told the departmental governor, Col. José Guevara M. that there was going to be trouble. "It was in the air," he recalled to Joaquín Méndez, Jr., "in the gestures and acts of individuals."

On the day of the election, a group of about two hundred leftists surrounded the government building in a menacing attitude. Acting quickly, the governor had the National Guard disarm them; ninety eight razor-sharp *corvos* were confiscated. ("This gave me the idea they were dangerous," the governor dryly remarked.) The communists "lost" the election, and of course, this made them more furious than ever. On January 4 there were disturbances in the *finca* of Santa Rita, eight kilometers due east of the town. The governor moved in troops and *guardia* who broke the back of the movement, although two soldiers and one trooper were killed.

However, rumors of an impending uprising continued to be heard. At first, reports circulated concerning a plan to assault the barracks of Ahuachapán on the twelfth; when that date passed without incident, it was rumored that the attack was postponed to the twenty-fourth. As the feeling of menace grew, wealthier citizens from the surrounding *fincas* began to push into Ahuachapán. The men presented themselves at the barracks, where they were hastily armed and instructed in the military arts. A part of this Civic Guard was kept at the barracks along with the regular military contingent, which consisted of some two hundred men composing the sixth infantry regiment.

The barracks of Ahuachapán was a grim, medieval-looking structure situated on a hill at the outskirts of town. It was of strong adobe construction, with crenellated battlements and Gothic towers with narrow windows. The gate was a formidable structure of stout wood reinforced with iron bars. Plainly, here was something which could be defended against anything short of artillery. But, according to Lt. Timoteo Flores, the garrison was disaffected from the government, having been contaminated by communist propaganda, and the Civic Guards were generally too green to be of any use. Just before the day of the attack, Capt. Vicente Hidalgo, commander of the machine gun detachment, had been arrested for his extremist views.[7] In another account, Col. Julio Calderón, who headed the military tribunal in Ahuachapán after the uprising, has stated that Major Miguel Angel Bolaños had found it necessary to disarm and expel many members of the regiment from the barracks. Those who remained were chiefly the members of the regimental band.[8]

The first alarm appears to have come about 10:00 P.M. on the twenty second. Some men approached the barracks and the guards at the gate fired into the air to frighten them off. The incident put the garrison on the alert. Shortly after this, the telegraph brought word of fighting in the vicinity of Sonsonate. Then, at 12:45 A.M., by Lt. Flores's account, three skyrockets rose over the bell tower of the church of San Francisco. They were later discovered to have been a signal to the rebels in the *barrio* of San Antonio to unite with the main body of rebels. The long-expected attack came at 1:30 on the morning of January 23. Some eight hundred men, according to on-the-spot estimates, came from the eastern *cantones* with another six hundred arriving from Atiquizaya and Turín to the northeast. These figures are probably exaggerated, but certainly, large numbers of men were involved. They came up to the wall of the barracks and attempted to smash through the gate or the walls with picks and crowbars. It was a hopeless undertaking. Well provided with automatic weapons, if not with trained men, Major Bolaños took a light machine gun and went from window to window raining fire down upon the attackers. They fled, but at 2:15 made a second attempt. Again a wall of lead greeted the assailants, but they fell back, regrouped and came on a third time against the few men in the barracks. Their tenacity was a great shock to the soldiers. Each attack was signalled in "Chinese" fashion with

7. 'Lt. Flores Narrative,' in Pineda, "Tragedia comunista," *Diario de Hoy,* February 9, 1967.
8. Julio Calderón, "Memorial histórico," p. 1.

blowing on *cuernos* or *caracol* shells and beating iron bars together.[9] At last they gave up and withdrew, but *La Prensa* stated on the twenty-sixth that another attack was made at 5:00 P.M. on the twenty-third.

While the main group of rebels assaulted the barracks in hopeless human waves and suffered high casualties, a group from the *barrio* San Antonio went into the town, which was cut off from the garrison and had little defense. About two in the morning they broke into the *alcaldía* and wrecked it, but then withdrew, when the barracks assault failed. No bourgeoisie were killed in the city.

But a party starting in the direction of the *finca* of San Juan del Conacaste, southwest of town, came across a dignified old man named Don Tobías Salazar, "a person esteemed for his age and social position," according to Jorge Schlesinger. Salazar had been warned that the communists were in Ahuachapán, but as a harmless old man, he felt that he had nothing to fear. He trusted in the fact that, like Redaelli, he was a known philanthropist and a friend of the poor.

Coming up to his horse, the mob began their depredations by removing the old gentlemen's shoes. He was then hauled off his horse and dragged along by the crowd. As they passed the coffee plantation of San Juan del Conacaste, the mob grew tired of their burden and so they pulled Salazar off the trail, in among the coffee plants, then ready for harvest. There they cut off his ears and nose and finally plunged a knife into his chest and through his heart.

Another person killed at the same location was Don Juan V. Germán. Francisco Romero had ridden out to warn him, but proved unable to budge his firm determination to remain on his *finca*. Romero barely made his getaway when the mob which had disposed of Salazar appeared and, before the eyes of his horrified family, put Germán to death in a hideous fashion. The chief perpetrator of the crime was a man named Juan Ramos, a servant and retainer of the family who had been Don Juan's companion from his youth and had even accompanied him to Guatemala when he went there to study. It was Ramos who led

9. Méndez, *Sucesos comunistas*, pp. 117-19.

the crowd to the plantation and supervised as they hacked various pieces off his old patron.[10]

Defeated in their efforts to take the departmental capital and fearing the arrival of a relief force, the rebels quickly abandoned the immediate area and crawled back into the rugged, twisted, overgrown hills that lie between Ahuachapán and Tacuba. The latter town, situated in one of the most remote valleys near the Guatemalan border, had been overrun at the start of the rebellion. The leading group among the local radicals were the Cuenca brothers, prominent Ladinos. Present in Tacuba at this time were Abel Antonio and his teen-aged brother Leopoldo. Efraín and Alfonso Cuenca were also involved in the fighting in the Ahuachapán area.

Tacuba was defended by only nine National Guards under the command of Major Carlos Juárez. These troopers panicked when they heard that there was going to be an uprising, and six of them deserted the major. Undaunted, the major and two noncommissioned officers tried to fight off the attackers from within the local guardpost. They fired until they ran out of ammunition as, time and again, waves of machete-wielding *campesinos* swarmed over the post. Finally, after all three *guardia* were seriously wounded, the post was overrun. The troopers were dragged out and the two NCOs murdered, after which their bodies were mutilated of "their noble parts," and the rebels "did obscene things which no mortal may relate."[11] Major Juárez was formally beheaded.

This was not the only resistance encountered in Tacuba. The local commandant was General Rafael Rivas, a crusty old soldier who had retired to Tacuba; now he found himself the object of a rebel attack. He had a pistol and blazed away as the door broke down. According to the later newspaper accounts he disposed of four *campesinos* before he was knocked down and seriously wounded. He was then dragged from his residence and, like the major, he was forced to kneel while his head was

10. Jorge Schlesinger, *Revolución comunista*, pp. 186-88; *La Prensa*, February 6, 1932.
11. Quote is from Lt. Flores, *Diario de Hoy*, February 9, 1967. Joaquín Méndez, Jr. gives the brave major's first name as Estanislao in *Sucesos comunistas*, pp. 128-29.

lopped off with a *corvo*. The head was then fastened to a pole and paraded through the streets of the town as a trophy. Later, when the rebels were overcome, the head could not be found, and the body of the fallen general had to be buried without it. Probably the ubiquitous pigs that roam the streets of Tacuba gobbled it up.

Col. Julio Calderón claims that there was at least one other victim of murder at Tacuba, an old man, "the father of Angélica V. de Fortín Magaña." The mob stripped him and put a rope around his neck, then made him crawl on all fours "with a ferocious *indiote* on his shoulders." Finally they decapitated him.[12]

Tacuba was in the hands of the rebels longer than any other major town, as government forces did not arrive until January 25. As a result, the leaders of the movement had a better chance to organize a real government. Abel Cuenca, aged twenty, who had been a university student in Guatemala City, was in charge of setting up the government. He forced the landholders to make numerous concessions to the rebels concerning the redistribution of the land and a fairer share of the region's wealth for the peasants. When he started, he had about eighteen hundred men under his command, but as the revolt failed elsewhere, the numbers of rebels in Tacuba swelled to five thousand. Food became a real problem and elaborate attempts were made to assure a fair distribution. To his credit, many say that he also worked to prevent further atrocities.

Despite all that happened at Ahuachapán and Tacuba, the one city which stands out in the popular imagination with Juayúa as a martyr to the revolt was Izalco. At the time, Izalco was the most Indian town of western El Salvador. It lies only eight kilometers from the departmental capital of Sonsonate, just off the main road to San Salvador. Turning northward from the highway, one must ascend a steep hill along the main street of the town. At the crest of the rise lies the parish church of Asunción, the "Indian" parish of Izalco. Isolated from the church proper is a bell tower which houses the massive bells

12. Julio Calderón, "Memorial historico," p. 3. This is the only record of this incident.

said to have been a gift from Charles V to the town in the sixteenth century. Looking back from Asunción, one can see the ocean clearly in the distance. In front of the church is a plaza, and on the other side, the *alcaldía*. Farther up the main street, with the volcano looming over its right shoulder, is the parish church of Dolores. In front of the Ladino church is another little park with an old bandstand and the *comandancia*, a ramshackle structure, on the other side. North of the town, up the slopes of Izalco, begin the coffee *fincas*. Today, Izalco, like almost every other town of any importance in El Salvador, is served by a system of buses running frequently, if off-schedule; the creaking and wheezing machines seem to be driven by failed Kamikaze pilots. In those days the road to the capital was a dirt track, and the most immediate link, besides the telegraph, to the outside world was a mule-drawn tramway that ran parallel to the road down to Sonsonate.

In Izalco, the leading radicals were José Feliciano Ama, the cacique of the Indian community, Eusebio Chávez, a Ladino carpenter, and his son Leopoldo. The Chávez family were "evangelicals" and highly respected in the community. Because of the agitation among the Indians, which had been going on now for almost a year, the citizens of Barrio Dolores had little doubt about the coming revolution. As early as December they had begun the formation of a civic guard among the non-Indian community, but they lacked arms and leadership to make their organization effective.

As a result of the January elections, a young, energetic man named Miguel Call had succeeded Rafael Carías Valdés as *alcalde*. Call became increasingly alarmed as the twenty-second approached; on the morning of that day he took a trip down to Sonsonate to beg the local *guardia* commander to restore the troopers, who had been removed a few days earlier when the National Guards were regrouped and concentrated. He received no satisfaction, however, and returned in the afternoon. That evening he was invited to eat with Rafael Castro Cárcamo to celebrate his election victory. After dinner, the two men were talking on the street in Barrio Asunción about three blocks west of the parish church, when they noticed a knot of men

153

approaching. As the men approached through the darkness, it could be seen that they were Indians and that they were armed with machetes. The mob, led by the cacique himself, surrounded the two townsmen. For a moment there was an uneasy confrontation. Then, the braver spirits among the rebels advanced with raised machetes and, at a given signal, began to hack at the two Ladinos, who tried to fend off the blows with their hands. After two or three minutes of flashing blades it was all over. The crowd recoiled in horror at what it had done. It left the still writhing bodies behind and went on toward Asunción.

According to his own recollections, Alfonso Díaz Barrientos came out of his house nearby and, aided by neighbors, dragged Miguel Call and Rafael Castro inside. The former expired almost at once, but Don Rafael, nursed by members of the household, lived until the rebellion was over and died several weeks later in a Sonsonate hospital. A temporary burial for the body of Miguel Call was arranged next door in the garden of Juan Hocking, for it was now impossible to leave the immediate area. Rampaging *campesinos* were running up and down the streets of Izalco, especially through Barrio Dolores, breaking into shops, liquor stores, and pharmacies. With a windup Victrola stolen from Francisco Alvarez, they began to make music and dance wildly about in drunken frenzy, having taken a quantity of alcohol from the store of Llort Hermanos. The parish priest of Asunción, Padre Castillo, who had considerable hold on his flock, tried to persuade them to moderate their conduct, and by morning they were more quiet. Despite the efforts of Ama and Eusebio Chávez, little constructive social revolution was accomplished and most of the time that the rebels spent in Izalco was given over to looting. That, rather than rape or murder, appears to have been the rule in Izalco as elsewhere.

The town was not entirely pacified. Díaz Barrientos had two or three rifles, and with these he climbed up to the roof of a neighboring house and forced the rebels to stay off his block by taking pot shots at anyone who came near. He remained up there for three days, sometimes assisted by a mysterious man he had never seen before, who came one night, dressed "as a carpenter," and aided him in his target practice. The man slipped away again before the troops arrived and no one ever learned his name.[13]

Many other leading citizens were forced to hide themselves in cellars and attics to escape the mob. Later, a number of these slipped out of town under cover of darkness and hid in the hills until the government retook the town on January 25. On the twenty-third, the government sent over an airplane which bombed the town. The projectiles fell in an already partially burned area, adding new devastation and causing a panic, not only among the rebels, but among the townspeople. The glow from fires set in Izalco could be seen clearly in Sonsonate, and everyone knew that it was only a question of time before an attempt would be made on that city.

13. The testimony of Alfonso Díaz Barrientos was taped by my colleagues Ernesto Sol Trujillo and Andrew J. Ogilvie.

Chapter 9

The Attack on Sonsonate and the Repression

Sonsonate was in the eye of the storm. All around the city the rebels were winning victories, but to control the western provinces of El Salvador it was absolutely essential to have this departmental capital. Sonsonate was, at that period, one of the most flourishing towns of El Salvador. Although it was the chief shopping center for the coffee growing region south of the *volcán*, the immediate area around the town was too low and too hot for coffee growing. Coconuts and tropical fruits flourished in the plain of Sonsonate, and large areas were and are devoted to cattle grazing. The city itself was noted for the elegance of its architecture. Arcades and verandas were common, to beat the steaming heat of the Sonsonate sun that often raised the temperature in July and August to over the hundred-degree mark. Here was no sleepy village, but a city of over twenty thousand souls, full of rich shops and stores waiting for the rebels to reach out and seize, or so it must have seemed.

For several days, ever since the announcement of Martí's capture, the population had lived in terror. There was ample evidence of what was going on around the city, but the troops of the departmental garrison, the eighth infantry, seemed unconcerned. People began to believe the rumor that they had been infiltrated by communists. Not even a picket was put out around the town.[1]

According to Major Castillo, an officer of the National Guard, a call was received from Izalco a little after midnight on the morning of the twenty-third, saying that the town (which had actually been overrun already) was being menaced by the

1. Pineda, "Tragedia comunista," *Diario de Hoy*, January 20, 1967.

Reds. In view of this, the army commander of the department, Col. Ernesto Bará, ordered Major Mariano Molina to organize a rescue brigade from among the eighth regiment before dawn the next morning.

The old *cuartel* of Sonsonate lay at the southeast end of the city, along the main road from Izalco to Acajutla, and along the railroad track, approximately at the place where the road from Nahulingo crosses it and turns into the main east-west street of Sonsonate. Not far away was a post of the Policía de Aduana, or customs police, manned by eleven well-armed troopers. There was also a post of *guardia* in the town and some Policía de Linea (now the National Police), as well as local policemen.

Before sunup, Molina paraded his troops in the plaza in front of the barracks, and began to requisition cars and trucks for the intended journey to Izalco. One car was sent off down the road to search out vehicles in the direction of Izalco. This car, however, ran directly into a huge mass of rebels coming toward Sonsonate. The driver and other occupants abandoned it and fled back on foot before the mob, who requisitioned the car and filled it with their own people. No sooner were the crowd of soldiers in the square than they saw the mob coming. The troops broke ranks and formed a ragged skirmish line, firing into the oncoming crowd of machete-wielding Indios. But the momentum of the assault was so great that the Reds were carried into the square, despite men falling right and left. A vicious hand-to-hand fight ensued, with bayonets and clubbed rifles clashing against machetes. There were about fifty soldiers in the square, and easily ten times that many rebels. The latter forced the soldiers to abandon the plaza and take refuge in the barracks, once again a medieval-type fort, from which the soldiers could fire more freely into their opponents. Some of the rebels got inside the gates with the troops, but these were dealt with handily. Over heaps of dead and wounded the rebels charged again and again at the doors and windows of the structure, only to be driven back by rifles and a couple of machine guns. Col. Bará himself directed the defense, although wounded in the hand by a machete.

Before reaching the barracks, the mob had broken into the customs house, taking the Policía de Aduana completely by surprise. In the dark interior of their quarters a bloody massacre followed. Corporal Gregorio Peñate and four troopers were hacked to death; the commanding officer, Mariano Guzmán, Corporal Francisco Martínez, and four privates managed to escape with their lives although all were wounded before they could fight their way out of the building. The dead bodies were taken outside and the usual outrages perpetrated on them. The mob seized a cache of arms in the building and used these weapons, although ineffectively, against the military barracks and the post of *guardia*. Racing down the street from the barracks, certain members of the rebel band, more intent on plunder than a fight, crossed the bridge over the Rio Grande de Sonsonate and penetrated as far as the central square of the town. There they broke into a couple of stores and set them afire, but there was no general sack of the town, for before long the superior firepower of the troops, *guardia*, and police began to tell. As the soldiers poured out of the barracks in pursuit of their fleeing opponents, the police units mopped up looters in the town. The invaders withdrew, leaving scores of their dead and wounded behind, and by 10:00 A.M. it was all over.

Rebel dead probably numbered between fifty and seventy. In addition to the Policía de Aduana, the government losses included four *guardia* killed and four wounded, one of whom later died of wounds. In addition, one soldier of the eighth regiment was killed and a number were wounded, including three officers. Two civilian drivers also died.[2]

A market woman afterwards recalled to Méndez her emotions during the attack. "When we heard the first shots we thought that our hour had come. The coming of the communist assault had been announced for several days, and we thought that when it happened no one over seven years of age would be left alive....They would kill us and burn our houses....But despite this, there was hardly a family which was not ready to defend

2. Méndez, *Sucesos comunistas*, pp. 11-12. Government losses are from *La Prensa*, January 26, 1932.

itself. In every house the fathers, mothers, even the children, expected at any moment to hear the first machete blows on the door. The families were armed with pistols, *corvos*, and other things."[3]

Although the rebel forces were driven out of Sonsonate by the troops, they lodged themselves securely in Sonzacate, which lies about two miles from the departmental capital just off the main road to Izalco. The town became a major communist stronghold. Here the leading figure among the rebels was a woman known as Comrade Julia, or "Red Julia." By the twenty-third there were an estimated five thousand rebels gathered there trying to decide whether to attempt another attack on Sonsonate or to await the coming of government forces.

After Sonsonate was secured, General Bará ordered a reconnaissance force under Colonel Tito Calvo to scout in the direction of Izalco. This unit, composed chiefly of National Guardsmen, ran into the strong Red force at Sonzacate and a fierce battle took place. Lt. Francisco Platero, directing the machine gun, and several of the soldiers were killed, along with a large number of their enemy. The troops were forced to retreat, taking their dead and wounded with them.[4]

Naturally, all these events had seriously alarmed the Martínez government. Acting as soon as word of the uprising reached the capital, the dictator named General José Tomás Calderón to put down the revolt. He was the same man who had visited Sonsonate in May of the previous year and had reported to Araujo on the state of affairs in the western departments. While Calderón was organizing his forces to move out against the rebels, the local citizenry were encouraged to form Civic Guards, units for defense of the local area, throughout western El Salvador. In every town where the communists were not in control these groups sprang into being. In Ahuachapán and Santa Ana, as well as in a few other spots, such units were already in the process of formation as early as December. Col. José Asencio Menéndez recalls that he was sent up to Santa Ana

3. Méndez, *Sucesos comunistas*, p. 10.
4. Pineda, "Tragedia comunista," *Diario de Hoy*, January 28, 1967.

a few days before the outbreak of fighting and met with coffee growers of the area in an attempt to organize them.

In San Salvador, Santa Ana, and other large centers, these Civic Guards grew numerous after the rebellion started. The composition of the *cívicos* varied. In some towns it is claimed that the units were made up chiefly of *señoritos*, while in larger cities they appealed to small shopkeepers and more prominent artisans. In general, every class that had something to lose by the success of the rebellion was represented in the Civic Guard. The equipment and uniform of these groups were heterogeneous. Each man had to supply his own outfit, including, in some cases, weapons. From photos I have seen, most of them appear to have been decked out to play in a jungle movie, with riding breeches, high boots, open-neck shirts, and a pith helmet or a wide-brimmed cowboy hat.

Outside of the fact that they freed more reliable units to go on patrol while they guarded the settled areas, the *cívicos* played very little part in the struggle. Legend attributes to them many of the massacres that followed the crushing of the revolt, but cooler heads discount these claims, giving dubious credit to the *guardia*. One interesting aspect of the Civic Guards was that, after the immediate repression was over, they became more like traditional *hermandades*, or religious brotherhoods, with masses, processions, and blessings, as well as military-style parades. In some respects these groups resembled the fascist units that sprang up under Mussolini and prefigured the later Falangists in Spain, with their emphasis on God and country, family and order. It is interesting to note in this respect that during the first hysteria following word of the rebellion, *La Prensa*, on January 27 and especially on January 28, can be seen calling for something much like a fascist state.

As the Civic Guards organized, government forces moved out from San Salvador and Santa Tecla to seize the area around Colón and clear the rebels from the department of La Libertad. At the same time, the besieged garrisons of Sonsonate and Ahuachapán began to strike back. Col. Marcelino Galdámez was given charge of the second expedition from Sonsonate. After hearing the report of Col. Calvo's fiasco, Galdámez started out on the morning of January 24, a Saturday. This time the government forces entered Sonzacate without a fight. Massive fires were burning in the town as the rebels had set fire to some oil storage tanks located there.

From Sonzacate, the expedition set off in army trucks and borrowed vehicles for Izalco. The drive on Izalco was also being undertaken from the direction of Colón, so that the enemy forces there were to be trapped between the two advancing units. Rather than immediately storming the town, the soldiers surrounded it and positioned themselves so that they would have a good cross fire when the rebels were smoked out. Obligingly, the rebel troops poured out of the town, down the hill toward the Sonsonate road, and into the mouths of the guns. Rifle and machine-gun fire cut them down in rows. Seeing the dead heaping up, José Feliciano Ama, "El Indio," ordered his forces to disband and to try to sneak away into the *volcán* region. Ama himself was captured in Izalco by the soldiers and taken to the *comandancia*, along with Leopoldo Chávez. Leopoldo's father, Eusebio, was among those who got away into the slopes of Izalco. The *comandancia* has an old cell facing the inner courtyard—a dark, dingy place with a barred door of heavy construction; in this hole Ama and Chávez were left. But the bourgeoisie of the town, having suffered a good deal from Ama, came to get him out and lynch him. The soldiers looked the other way.

Alfonso Rochac, a reporter, claimed in a story that appeared in *La Prensa* on February 2, 1932, that he talked to Ama just before he was hanged. He described the old Indian as having been a prominent landholder who "always dressed well." He added that during the rebellion Ama had worn a red tie. Rochac asked him why he had led the revolt, and he claimed that Ama replied that he had done no such thing. "You know me. I'm a pacifist. I had nothing to do with the revolt. I was in my house when they found me." Asked who else was in the revolt, the old chief said, "I don't know their names and didn't see them." He repeated this when he was taken to the park, photographed, and then hanged. The hanging of Ama and of Leopoldo Chávez took place in the little square opposite the church of Asunción, on olive trees which have since been removed. According to the present cacique of Izalco, a close personal friend of Ama, who escaped involvement in the rebellion because he had been arrested at Coatepeque before the revolt, Rochac's account omits the fact that, as Ama was being brought to the park from the *comandancia* (which is on the square across from the church of Dolores, about half a mile away), he was slapped around so much that he was dead by the time the citizens hanged him. This does not seem unlikely, for he was not greatly loved by the people of the town.

Another grim detail, from *La Prensa*, was that the rope broke twice as they were trying to hang Leopoldo Chávez. Postcard-size photographs of Ama hanging, with his name written on in white ink, were sold in El Salvador after the rebellion, along with other equally gruesome photos of the counterrevolution.

Eusebio Chávez, although wounded, got as far as Santa Ana, where he sought refuge in the house of another son. There he was picked up by police of the line on February 3. The police, under the command of Col. J. Mariano Castellanos, had to struggle with Chávez's son, who shot and wounded one of the agents. The papers on the fourth also said that Federíco Delgado, a prominent leader of the revolt, had been picked up at Nueva Concepción (Chalatenango) on the same date. Eusebio Chávez was executed the same day he was captured, as was Delgado.

After making sure that Izalco was in friendly hands, the majority of the troops, under Col. Galdámez, set out for Nahuizalco, arriving about 5:30 P.M. According to the account of José Mariano Alarcón (a civilian driver requisitioned by the expedition), just as they were arriving at the point where the Sonsonate-to-Juayúa road has a turnoff to Nahuizalco, the troops ran into several carloads of rebels heading in the direction of Sonsonate. The government forces halted the rebel caravan and a sharp fight followed which lasted about thirty minutes. The Reds were supplied with arms, probably Araujo's Mausers, and battled tenaciously before they were at last routed. Several vehicles were destroyed in the crossfire. After the enemy had fled into the ravines in the area, the troops proceeded into Nahuizalco, where they met no further resistance.[5]

The next day, Sunday, January 25, the government forces proceeded to Juayúa. It was there that the rebel forces had decided to make their stand. The roads leading to the town had been barricaded with cut down trees, and the rebels had made trenches to defend the town. In some places these had been dug across the road and covered with leaves in the hope that the government vehicles might plunge into them. All things considered, it must have been slow going toward Juayúa.

After hand-to-hand fighting around the outposts, the government forces slowly occupied the town and sent Francisco (Chico) Sánchez heading for the hills. With a few followers, the rebel leader circled around the government troops and made for San Pedro Puxtla, some miles to the south. He was not caught until about February 15. Then he was brought back to Juayúa and faced a firing squad; Chico Sánchez wept bitterly for forgiveness. A number of other leading rebels from the Juayúa area were captured, including José Domingo Mate and his father, Juan, who were captured and executed after the battle, and Rafael Borjas, Nicolás Sánchez, and Rasalio Nerio, later named as the man most responsible for the murder of the commandant, Col. Vaquero.[6]

Although the Red forces were driven out of Nahuizalco and Juayúa, they continued to be active in the area for several days. Col. Francisco Salinas, commanding the National Guard troops in the area, reported sniping and rock throwing along the road between Nahuizalco and Juayúa.

While troops from Sonsonate pacified that department, a column set forth on the twenty-fifth from Ahuachapán with orders to retake Tacuba. The group was led by Major Saturnino Cortez and consisted of about fifty to eighty National Guards, and a Hotchkiss machine-gun crew. According to Lt. Flores, they arrived about 5 P.M. the same day. "Major Cortez attacked from the east side of the town, by a place known as Las Pirámides. It was not possible to follow the access road to Tacuba because it

5. Méndez, *Sucesos comunistas*, pp. 73-74.
6. Ibid., pp. 74-75.

was barricaded by the communists. There was an enormous slaughter when the machine gun fired rapidly and the bands of communists attacked in wave on wave, crying savagely."[7]

The guiding spirit of the defense of Tacuba was Abel Cuenca, a twenty-year-old university student, along with his younger brother Leopoldo. To defend themselves against the government forces, the rebels in Tacuba had about one hundred Mauser rifles, taken from the National Guard post when the town was seized, and a few other assorted firearms for their five thousand men. The fight lasted two and a half hours. Some houses and fields caught fire and a number of dead and wounded *campesinos* were burned. The government troops were victorious, and, moving into the peasant sections of the town, they flushed out the surviving rebels by the simple expedient of setting fire to their huts and shooting them as they came out. It is said that a large number of those killed by the troops were women and children. Leopoldo Cuenca, Jr., was captured at his mother's house, wounded, and dispatched with three shots by Col. Francisco Rivas.[8]

One reason for the fury of the soldiers may have been the rumor that on the night of the twenty-fifth, the rebels had been planning a mass violation of the women of Tacuba, "regardless of age or condition."[9] This story resembles the tale which was told in Juayúa, and may or may not be true. It is perhaps significant that such a *noche de bodas* was always going to take place on the very night of the day that the troops arrived. It would have been out of character for Abel Cuenca to have allowed such a thing. Certainly, however, a number of atrocities had been committed, and the bourgeois citizens and the military had every reason to feel revengeful against the peasant masses.

A number of members of the Cuenca family took part in the revolt in the western provinces. Efraín Cuenca, who had been in the area but was not with Abel and Leopoldo, was captured by Ubico's troops just after crossing the Guatemalan border

7. "Lt. Flores Narrative," in Pineda, "Tragedia comunista," *Diario de Hoy*, February 10, 1967.
8. Buezo, *Sangre de Hermanos*, pp. 94-96.
9. "Lt. Flores Narrative," in Pineda, "Tragedia comunista," *Diario de Hoy*, February 10, 1967.

and was turned over to the Salvadoreans. He was brought to Tacuba and hanged in the bell tower of the church on January 30. Alfonso Cuenca was captured deep in Guatemalan territory; General Ubico, in one of his strange fits of black humor, ordered him marched on foot back the way he had come to the Salvadorean border. There he was turned over to the authorities and was shot, along with his friend Hércules Martínez, on February 19. Abel Cuenca made it across the border on foot in forty-eight hours. There he found and "borrowed" a mule, and rode on to Guatemala City. From there he got away to Honduras, but the Hondurans discovered him and imprisoned him for communist activity. After his release in the 1940s, he went back to Guatemala; there he served in the government under Jacobo Arbenz Guzmán, being a prominent official of that president's political party. After the debacle of '54 he went to Chile, visited El Salvador clandestinely during Lemus's presidency, and was finally amnestied by a special act of the legislature in 1968. Still another brother, Dr. Max Ricardo Cuenca, a chemist, was a leader in the revolutionary movement in San Salvador. He escaped to Honduras, and thence to the Soviet Union, where he studied for three years. He then returned to Honduras and, like Abel, went to the aid of Arbenz. With the collapse of that regime he moved to Chile and died there by suicide in 1965. Their father was also implicated in the movement and faced a firing squad at Nahuizalco after being captured in Sonsonate. Another brother, as Sr. Cuenca wryly told me, "did not take part in politics."[10]

In addition to all the rebel leaders mentioned above, most of the prominent chiefs of the movement met death within a few days. According to a document in my possession, Miguel Mármol and Rafael Bondanza were brought to San Salvador and turned over to the National Police on January 30. Shortly afterwards they were shot at Soyapango, Bondanza crying at the moment of his death, "Viva la Internacional Comunista."[11]

10. Buezo, *Sangre de Hermanos*, pp. 97-102, as amplified and corrected in conversations with Abel Cuenca.
11. De la Selva, "Lucha," p. 214; but, according to Osmín Aguirre papers, the execution could not have taken place on January 27 as this writer

But Salvadorean firing squads have notoriously poor marksmanship, and Miguel Mármol, with four bullet wounds in him, managed to crawl away in the dark. Later, in Guatemala, he gave Pedro Geoffroy Rivas the story of his escape. He hid out in the hills near the capital several days and at last slipped into his mother's house. His mother had erected a family altar in the parlor and was praying for the soul of the dead son when he entered. She hid him behind the same altar, where for several days he was edified by his friends' prayers for his repose. Later, he escaped from the country. He now lives in Mexico City.[12]

Inocente Rivas Hidalgo, the student leader, was also captured after the revolt, but the prominence of his family saved him from execution. He was allowed to slip quietly into exile, moving to London, where he became a lawyer. He died in England in 1968.

Joaquín Rivas, Ismael Hernández, and most of the other prominent communists were done away with as well, but there were still a number of persons hiding in the hills after January 25. The government remained wary. There was an attempt to take San Antonio Abad, on the outskirts of the capital, on January 24, and a disturbance in the city of Santa Ana, which had remained quiet during the main revolt, on January 28. On February 18 about three hundred Indian peasants again seized Nahuizalco and held it for a day, but the government quickly counter-attacked and drove them off with heavy casualties. From February 20 to 24 there was a serious alarm in the area of Sonzacate, outside Sonsonate, but nothing major came of it and the rebels were dispersed before they could take offensive action.[13]

The Guatemalan frontier was the scene of some nervousness on two counts. For one thing, the government of El Salvador

states, because there is a document accepting Bondanza and Mármol at police headquarters in San Salvador on January 30.
12. Geoffroy Rivas himself had written for *Estrella Roja*, and was among those slated for extermination. However, the French connections of this family saved him and he slipped away to Guatemala where he met Mármol, and worked during the period of Arévalo and Arbenz.
13. Méndez, *Sucesos comunistas*, pp. 16-17.

daily expected a *Laborista* attack from that direction. *La Prensa* on January 27 falsely reported that Luis Felipe Recinos had been killed leading a force of Araujo's followers into El Salvador. The tension was eased when Ubico, about this time, expelled his old friend Araujo from the country, along with Recinos and Masferrer.

On the other hand, the Guatemalan government was closely guarding the border, because it expected a mass invasion of communists from El Salvador. The Guatemalan press on February 1 announced that large groups of men had crossed the border the previous day and were preparing an uprising. Actually, the rebels who did make it to Guatemala were a pretty bedraggled lot and it seems unlikely that the state was in danger. Ubico remained in power until 1944, the same year that Martínez fell.

The "Yankee Imperialists," against whom the rebellion was supposedly aimed, had not stood idly by while the communists tried to seize the country. The chargé d'affaires in the capital, W. J. McCafferty (not to be confused with special envoy Jefferson Caffery), informed his government at once concerning the gravity of the situation. As a result of his dispatch, several U.S. and Canadian vessels cruising in Pacific waters near El Salvador were ordered to make for the stricken country. They arrived on January 25. The group included the cruiser U.S.S. *Rochester*, the U.S. destroyers *Wickes* and *Philips*, and the Canadian destroyers *Vancouver* and *Skeena*. The two U.S. destroyers dropped anchor at La Libertad, and the commander of the squadron, Rear Admiral Arthur St. Clair Smith, radioed to General Calderón asking if the U.S. and Canadian forces should land Marines and armed sailors to back up the government.

That was the last thing that General Calderón, or the dictator Martínez, wanted. To their minds, the idea of Yankee intervention was only a shade less frightening than that of a communist uprising. The Marines were just then getting out of neighboring Nicaragua, and their record of long-term intervention in Honduras, the Dominican Republic, Haiti, and Cuba made them unwelcome guests anywhere in Latin America.

It could easily be recalled by the Salvadoreans that several of the interventions mentioned above had started from a similar necessity of maintaining order. General José Tomás Calderón therefore wired back indignantly that he needed no help and that the rebellion was already crushed. Here, however, a first-class confusion took place. The general radioed that the revolt was under control and "four thousand, eight hundred communists have been liquidated." These grim tidings were promptly reported to the world press, which depicted a counterrevolutionary blood bath and white terror. At this Calderón was quite angry. When Joaquín Méndez, Jr., interviewed him a couple of days later, he said, "I have learned that my dispatch from Acajutla has been misinterpreted in some countries. When I spoke of the number of communists liquidated they took it to mean the number killed. To clarify this I have sent a telegram to all the newspapers in this country as follows: 'Ahuachapán, February 3, 1932. I have seen published in various periodicals the statement which says that four thousand, eight hundred communists were killed—a statistic which is not correct. In the laconic message which was sent from Acajutla as a salute to the commander of the warships, I said four thousand, eight hundred liquidated; that is to say, broken totally and dislocated in their diabolic plots'"[14] That explanation would clarify a great deal, except that it appears that the general (who was one of El Salvador's leading social scientists and statisticians) was not being quite candid. His statement that so many were liquidated probably was meant to signify so many killed, until the horrified reactions of the foreign press came in, at which time the wording was changed to "broken and dislocated." On the other hand, the general was probably exaggerating his own prowess as a communist-killer, and it hardly seems likely that he could have disposed of so many in such a few days.

Exactly what was going on in El Salvador after the crushing of the rebellion? To answer this question one must first of all understand the mood of the bourgeoisie and the army in the country. They had sensed for a long time dark rumblings among

14. Ibid.

the masses of the people, as the plantation owners of the Old South must have sensed them. In the rebellion of January, 1932, their worst fears had been realized. Indian and peasant discontent had been linked to the dread specter of International Communism. It is hardly surprising that their actions against the now doubly "red" Indians were hysterical and violent. Guillermo Herrador Tejada must have spoken for many Salvadoreans of the upper classes when he wrote, in *Diario Latino* on February 4, a denunciation of the government for its previous leniency toward "the criminal elements," and demanded that the government take away even machetes from the common people.

This being the mood of the people who now had the upper hand, the *matanza,* or massacre, which now took place, can hardly be surprising. Around Izalco a roundup of suspects began. As most of the rebels, except the leaders, were difficult to identify, arbitrary classifications were set up. All those who were found carrying machetes were guilty. All those of a strongly Indian cast of features, or who dressed in a scruffy, *campesino* costume, were considered guilty. To facilitate the roundup, all those who had *not* taken part in the uprising were invited to present themselves at the *comandancia* to receive clearance papers. When they arrived they were examined and those with the above mentioned attributes seized. Tied by the thumbs to those before and behind them, in the customary Salvadorean manner, groups of fifty were led to the back wall of the church of Asunción in Izalco and against that massive wall were cut down by firing squads. In the plaza in front of the *comandancia,* other selected victims were made to dig a mass grave and then shot, according to one account, with machine guns mounted on trucks. In some cases, women and children refused to leave their menfolk and shared their fate.[15] An old Izalco resident, who was then a soldier in the army, says that there is

15. Bustamante, *Historia militar*, p. 106; Darwin J. Flakoll and Claribel Alegría, *Cenizas de Izalco* (Barcelona, 1966), p. 164. This novel, which has considerably more literary merit than *Ola roja*, gives a graphic account of the Izalco massacre.

no doubt that the *guardia* behaved much worse than the rebels, "shooting anyone they came across."

In Juayúa, the government authorities played the same trick as in Izalco, ordering the peasants to appear for a safe conduct and then killing men, women, and children, and "even the little dogs which followed their masters," according to one account.[16] Similar incidents took place all over the western part of the country, from Turín to Acajutla and from Tacuba to Ilopango, and even at such isolated spots in the east as Jiquilisco. In Tacuba people still point out a group of sulfur pits near the town where they say the bodies of the victims were buried.

The roadways were littered with bodies in many areas, the drainage ditches along the side serving as expeditious burial places. In some cases burial was too shallow or nonexistent and "the pigs and buzzards ate well for a while," as one person interviewed put it. How many died at any particular place is impossible to say, but an educated historian, well informed on local affairs, and an old Indian resident of the town both gave me the figure of two thousand in Nahuizalco alone—a figure which is perhaps too high, but testifies to the fact that no small number were executed.

Recently an old man came forward with his story of the *matanza* in Nahuizalco.[17] He was a *campesino*, Dionisio Nerio. According to his story, he was traveling through Colón when the rebels attacked and forced him to join them. He went with them for some distance toward Santa Tecla but then managed to slip away and scurried home toward Nahuizalco. Along the road he passed groups of rebels trying to break down the doors of houses and, it seemed to him, killing anyone they came across. Each group, he noted, had a red and black flag. He arrived in Nahuizalco on January 25, a day after the government troops. There Nerio remained at peace until the thirteenth of February. On that day Capt. Flores Argumedo, the military commander of

---

16. Bustamante, *Historia militar*, p. 106. This historian is not completely reliable, but this picture is, I believe, accurate.
17. "Fusilado relata episodio de 1932," *Diario de Hoy*, May 11, 1969. It will be noted that the *fusilado* has the same last name as several of the Nahuizalco ringleaders, a circumstance which may have had something to do with his "execution."

the town, sent out an order that all those who did not have safe-conduct passes were to come to the *comandancia,* where the necessary papers would be issued. As Nerio had been out of town when the troops entered, he had no pass.

When he presented himself at the military headquarters along with several hundred other men, he was arrested with the rest. That evening they were led out to be shot in batches of eight men at a time, tied thumb-to-thumb. The firing squad of only six soldiers had to fire several rounds to account for all eight, who were then allowed to tumble backward on top of the last batch in a mass grave. Nerio, unscathed, lay in the pit for some hours as shots rang out and more bodies were tossed in. At last, using his teeth, he cut the bonds that held him to the neighboring corpses and crawled away in the dark. He managed to get away to the *finca* of his *patrón,* who sheltered him until the *matanza* was well over. For what it is worth, he claims that 985 *campesinos* were in the group rounded up and shot on the thirteenth alone.

Col. Julio C. Calderón, the brother of the general in charge of the pacification, conducted the military tribunal at Ahuachapán. According to his own account,[18] he presided over the trial, and, one must presume, the execution of 250 "communists" there. In justification of the government he recites the very real crimes of the rebels and asks: "Before such crimes who could fold their arms? No, no, that couldn't be, those who were captured were so fierce, and they paid for their crimes in the same places where they slew their victims." A part of those he tried were military defectors from the local garrison.

One curious incident that he related in regard to the trials in Ahuachapán was the arrival on the scene of a Spanish Dominican priest with letters from Martínez and the archbishop of San Salvador saying that he was to be allowed to talk to the prisoners. Col. Calderón, expecting an edifying sermon, assembled the condemned men, but the priest began: "Brothers, you are not at fault and you shouldn't be here, on the bench of the accused, but rather the bourgeoisie of Ahuachapán, masters of estates, *fincas, haciendas,* and mines." Colonel Calderón

18. Julio Calderón, "Memorial histórico," pp. 1-2, 4-5.

ordered him to get out of the *cuartel*. Later the same priest tried to make trouble by accusing the colonel of being a theosophist, like the dictator. Only after several days of negotiations did the army persuade the Dominican to decamp.

Not all the massacres took place out in the countryside. Using the voting lists, authorities in San Salvador rounded up all those who had voted Communist, or who were suspect for other reasons. Many of these people were the victims of personal vengeance. "Every night trucks went full of victims from the Dirección General de Policía to the banks of the Rio Acelhuate where the victims were shot out of hand and buried in great ditches without even their names being taken."[19]

Joaquín Castro Canizales has given us a vivid account of the events in the capital:

> Martial law...was applied excessively in the cities. How many vengeances took place on that occasion! A mere joke against so-and-so was enough to send one to the cells of the *policía* and thence to oblivion. An employee of Don Juan Lüders, owner of "El Fénix," was killed taking a little house dog for a walk, and two boys in El Coro, who went to bathe early in the morning, were cut down by the *cívicos*.
>
> That martial law of 1932 ended forever the gay life of the city—on starry nights boys serenading romantic girls, student bands such as Los Cheros or Guanatica, or *marimbas* called *ticuiseras* roaming about....It converted the capital into a cemetery....No one went out because of fear. [20]

This from the man whose coup put Martínez in power!

Buezo claims that in some instances hotels and hostels were invaded and those who had blond hair were dragged out and killed as suspected Russians.[21] But it should be noted that there is no record of any North American being killed by the government.

19. Bustamante, *Historia militar*, p. 106.
20. Quino Caso, "Acontecimientos," *Tribuna Libre*, January 25-26, 1952.
21. Buezo, *Sangre de hermanos*, p. 67.

Just how many persons were killed in the *matanza* will never be known. Certainly General Martínez had few scruples about the killings. In this he appears to have been aided by his bizarre religious views. He called his cult Theosophy, and he said that it taught him that "it is a greater crime to kill an ant than a man, for when a man dies he becomes reincarnated, while an ant dies forever."[22] During the revolt itself, one of his aids reproached him about the ferocity of the repression and he answered by quoting an Indian religious text (probably the *Bhagavad Gita*) to the effect that he did not kill with malice, but dispassionately. "I am only the instrument of the fates to fulfill destiny."[23]

However, as *Opinión Estudiantil* suggested on July 8, 1944, just after his overthrow, more practical motivation might have had more to do with his actions than any religious impulse. Martínez may have been trying to pose before world opinion, especially that of the United States, as the champion of anti-communism.

As far as total figures are concerned, estimates vary greatly. Salvadoreans, like medieval people, tend to use numbers like fifty thousand simply to indicate a great number—statistics are not their strong point. López Vallecillos says that sixteen thousand persons took part in the uprising and that forty thousand were killed. Mauricio de la Selva puts the figure at thirty thousand killed by the government. Jorge Schlesinger says twenty-five thousand, while Colonel Bustamante gives twenty-four thousand. Rudolfo Buezo claimed that he saw government figures which put the total at twenty thousand; Dr. David Luna accepts this figure also.[24]

However, sources who might have had a better opportunity to judge suggest lower figures. Joaquín Castro Canizales told me that sixteen thousand would be about right. Osmín Aguirre, who commanded the *policía*, says that the number executed did not exceed six or seven thousand, and General Salvador Peña Trejo

22. Martz, *Central America*, p. 82.
23. This story was told to me by journalist Serafín Quiteño.
24. López Vallecillos, *El periodismo*, p. 106; de la Selva, "Lucha," p. 196; Jorge Schlesinger, *Revolución comunista*, p. 4; Bustamante, *Historia militar*, p. 107; Buezo, *Sangre de hermanos*, pp. 84-86; Luna "Tragico suceso," p. 63.

says two or three thousand were killed. He too was in a position to know, as he was in charge of organizing the Civic Guard in much of the area covered by the revolt. Miguel Pinto, Jr., the publisher of *Diario Latino*, seems to think this last figure is valid.

Of course, it might be suggested that some of the lower estimates have been motivated by partisan considerations. Rollie Poppino, who touches on the subject in his general study of Latin American communism, accepts twenty-five thousand.[25] But I must admit that I think that this figure is too high simply because of the physical problems involved in getting rid of such a large number of people in so short a time. The number of troops and police on hand, the amount of ammunition and time which they had, and the numbers who would have been foolish enough to fall into their hands, seem to suggest something more like eight to ten thousand as a reasonable estimate.

Casualty figures for the other side are equally hard to come by. The government never released a full figure on the number of civilians killed, nor the number of military personnel. Recently, I went with the director of the National Archives to see the chief of staff of the army, only to be told that the records no longer existed! However, approximate figures are not so hard to ascertain for the government side as for the rebels. The present work tabulates twenty-one persons, including local police, but excluding the *guardia*, police of the line, customs police, and soldiers, killed in the uprising by the rebels. At the major centers of the revolt I tried to gather from as many persons as possible their recollections of numbers killed and this figure was the largest I could come up with. There are one or two possible confusions of names, and it is further possible that I might have missed as many as eight or ten citizens killed, but certainly the total number of those who fell to the machetes and guns of the rebels could not have been more than thirty-five.[26]

25. Rollie E. Poppino, *International Communism in Latin America: A History of the Movement, 1917-1963.* (New York: Free Press, 1964), p. 141.
26. This is a far cry from the "hundreds of landowners and merchants" that Poppino says were slaughtered (ibid., p. 142).

As to military casualties, five men of the Policía de Aduana were killed in the attack on Sonsonate. There is no record of other customs police being killed. Col. Osmín Aguirre y Salinas himself tells me that his Policía de Linea lost no more than ten killed, including six at Sonsonate and three in Santa Tecla. Five *guardia* died at Sonsonate, and three more at Tacuba. *La Prensa* gave a list of all the National Guards killed in the uprising, in its issue of February 6, 1932, numbering only nine names, with ten others wounded. Leaving plenty of room for error, it is hardly possible that more than thirty men from all the paramilitary police organizations were killed in the rebellion.

Regular army figures do not come so easily. Peña Trejo suggests around a hundred soldiers and police combined, while Castro Canizales, who was in an equally good position to know, being an officer at the military school and close to the regime, says only a few soldiers were killed. Considering these opinions, and including the soldiers executed as traitors among the rebels, a top estimate of the number of soldiers killed would be about forty. Half that many might be more accurate.

Taking all these figures, it appears that the rebels killed about one hundred persons altogether during the uprising; about ten thousand rebels may have lost their lives afterwards in the *matanza* or in the course of the fighting, with easily 90 percent falling in the *matanza*. This means that the government exacted reprisals at the rate of about one hundred to one. Further, one can see that the number of persons killed in the uprising amounted to about .7 percent of the total population of El Salvador, a not inconsiderable figure.

The revolt, launched in blood, had ended in even greater bloodshed. It would be pointless to argue whether or not the atrocities committed by the revolutionaries justified those committed by the government. Both sides believed that everything was at stake and that any means would be justified. The result for the already depressed nation of El Salvador was incalculable.

The revolt was over by January 25, for all practical purposes, and the *matanza* was well under way by that date. But one last act of the drama of 1932 had yet to be played, and it was this final act which caught the imagination of the Salvadoreans more than anything which had gone before.

Chapter 10

The Trial and Execution of Martí Luna, and Zapata

The Old Penitentiary in San Salvador was wrecked by an earthquake in the 1960s, and the site is now a vacant lot. But on January 19, 1932, the doors of the old building closed on Martí, Luna, and Zapata. It is difficult to imagine what Augustín Farabundo Martí, veteran of so many misadventures and imprisonments, might have thought. Having survived so often, he probably expected that his coolness and moral superiority would bring him unscathed through those penitentiary doors again. But he was destined not to leave them until February 1, 1932, when he went to his execution with Mario Zapata and Alfonso Luna.

In the course of the interrogations which followed his capture, Martí gradually became aware that the revolt had taken place and that it had failed. Neither the uprising nor its failure would have surprised him. As René Padilla rightly remarked, this revolt was his last card, and he knew it.

Outside the prison, there was constant speculation that the three conspirators had been shot against a wall of the fortress-like building. With so many rebels being executed out of hand, it seemed hard to believe that the government would bother to go through any legal formalities with the man believed to be most responsible for the bloodshed; but General Hernández Martínez knew perfectly well what he was doing. He set out to make Martí a legendary folk villain, and by and large succeeded, through holding a publicized trial and condemnation. The execution of the three prisoners would bring the rebellion to an end on a perfect note of tragedy and finality.

For Martí's young associates, prison was a new experience. Mario Zapata had been married less than a year and was about to become a father at the time of his arrest. His wife, Doña Nieves Cea de Zapata, had been harassed by the government between the time of the suppression of *Estrella Roja* and the actual capture of her husband. She had been repeatedly ordered to disclose his whereabouts, but refused.[1]

At the end of the rebellion, the three prisoners were told that they would be tried before a "council of war"—that is, a court-martial. They were urged to give whatever evidence they had to the government concerning others responsible for the uprising, but they refused. Buezo pictures Martí as declaring, "We are not cowards....We will not dishonor ourselves."[2] They were then asked who they wanted for their attorneys. A number of names were suggested by the defendants, and in the end the post was given to a young fourth-year law student, René Padilla Velasco, now an official of the Ministry of Foreign Affairs. From talking to him I gather that he accepted the defense of all three men rather reluctantly, out of a sense of duty rather than from any basic sympathy to the rebel cause. He had been a classmate of Luna and Zapata and knew them fairly well.

The council of war, according to *Diario Latino*,[3] consisted of the following members: General Manuel Antonio Casteñeda, president, and Colonel Hipólito Ticas, General Emilio Marroquín Velásquez, Col. Domingo García Morán, and Col. Ladislao Escobar. The secretary was Dr. Arturo Salano, and General Eléazar López was prosecutor. Lieutenant Castro Canizales was also present as a secretary to the court. The trial was convened at 6:00 P.M. on January 30, 1932, in a meeting room at the penitentiary. After the members had been installed in office, the reading of the case commenced at seven o'clock. This went on until eleven. Then, without recess, the arguments commenced and continued until 1:00 A.M.

---

1. Buezo, *Sangre de hermanos*, pp. 70-71.
2. Ibid, pp. 73-74.
3. The account of the trial and execution is from the press of February 1, 1932, especially *Diario Latino* and *La Prensa*, except where noted.

When the prosecutor had finished his presentation, Alfonso Luna begged the court for an opportunity to speak on his own behalf. This was granted, and the young man began in a somewhat trembling tone to explain that his activity in the communist movement was nothing but a kind of foolishness, the action of an enthusiastic youth who did not anticipate the tragic consequences of his actions. He explained that he and Mario Zapata were but two boys who, in a period of rebelliousness and madness, had joined the communists only as sympathizers to their cause and not as real members. Their sympathy sprang from their belief that the moment had come to do justice for the peasants and proletariat, but they never believed that to do justice it would be necessary to commit actions so inhuman as those which the court attributed to the communist mob. As to their presence with Martí at the house in San Miguelito, they had come, obeying a fatal impulse, because they had been told that if they were caught they would be deported from the country for having dared to publish *Estrella Roja;* since they were afraid of possible deportation, they had come to seek counsel and comfort from Martí, whom they considered their master. When they went there they were ignorant of what was planned and had not meant to link themselves to this bloody and subversive movement. Luna ended his oration by saying that they were both innocent as far as the uprising was concerned, and that as editors of *Estrella Roja* they had praised the coup of December 2, only advising General Martínez that the time had now come to do justice to the masses. All Luna's testimony was, of course, quite true, as every informed person I spoke to in El Salvador has readily admitted, but it made little impression on the court, which was determined to see the three prisoners executed.

Zapata was then allowed to speak. Although thin and haggard-looking, he was steady and composed. He denied that he was a communist, explaining that his position as a semi-bourgeoisie, semi-intellectual made it difficult for him to gain acceptance into the communists' ranks. As for the documents that the prosecution had brought in to link him to the movement, they related only to some articles which were to be published in

Estrella Roja. The two student leaders, Zapata claimed, had only become closely linked to the party with the publication of the paper in December. On the other hand, he could hardly deny his well known activity for FRTS, for radical student movements, and for the popular university. The court listened impassively as he declared, "We are figures of the second rank." This was true; it was obvious; but it made no difference. The country was in a mood for vengeance, especially against the young rebels of the university. The court was in no mood for nice distinctions. Last, the defendant Agustín Farabundo Martí was given a chance to speak. It was now after midnight. The meeting room of the court, really nothing more than the largest room of the commandant's apartment, was ill-lit and dismal. Martí rose, looking, in the words of *La Prensa,* "visibly moved, with a nervous tic causing an old scar on his forehead to twitch." He began by putting the court on trial, pointing out that this was in reality the trial of one class by another. Since he was already guilty, according to public opinion, as the leader of the communists, he would not bother to deny it, but accepted full responsibility for what had happened. However, he begged the court to realize that the students Luna and Zapata were not deeply implicated. They were not communists, having no foundation in Marxism, nor any proletarian consciousness. They were simply middle-class idealists who had looked upon himself, Martí, as their teacher.

At one o'clock the court recessed and the three were returned to their cells while the judges began their debate. The prisoners passed what has been described as a "tranquil night."[4] Martí lay smoking on his mat, lost in thought, or perhaps trying not to think. (It has been claimed that the bachelor revolutionary was enamored of a married lady of about thirty whom he had known since he was a student, and although he never spoke of it, this frustrated passion remained strong to the end.) [5]

Luna spent the night talking with a priest who had come to visit him. Zapata paced nervously up and down, stroking his prison-grown beard. At last, at 6:30, they were summoned back

4. Pineda, "Tragedia comunista," *Diario de Hoy,* February 7, 1967.
5. Buezo, *Sangre de hermanos,* pp. 55-56.

to the courtroom. It is doubtful that the judges had debated all night. Probably they all retired to their homes or slept in the penitentiary, for in truth, there was little to discuss. General Maximiliano Hernández Martínez had already given the sign.

The court read the verdict that all the prisoners were guilty and would meet death by firing squad the next morning for their crimes of treason and rebellion. When the reading was finished, Luna turned to Martí and said in a loud voice, "Martí is as Plato. I recognize in him my master." And then he asked, "Do you recognize me as your pupil?"

The veteran of the Segovias and a thousand bloody strikes looked at the sincere young student for a moment without speaking. Perhaps not without a trace of irony, he replied, "Yes, I recognize you, my disciple." Then, in a perkier tone, he added, "And now we go to die, we three together."

On the thirty-first the prisoners were allowed to receive visitors, but after all, most of their friends had already gone before a firing squad, or were in prison or in hiding. Two ladies, Concha and Elvira Ayala, came and spoke with them, doubtless giving the prisoners many details about the *matanza*. In the afternoon they were herded into the chapel for a service, and afterwards two priests arrived, Fathers Prieto and Rutilio Montalvo. Martí said that he had no sins to confess, but the two students made their peace with God.

In Buezo's narration, Martí told the priest that he had ceased to believe in those "omnipotent principles which, according to you people, are all justice and all love." He asked the priest, "Do you believe that the social conditions of our country are just?" He pointed out that the church had worked with the state to enslave the Salvadorean people, and had participated in the recent massacres. "Are the killings that the military and the bourgeoisie have committed on our ranks just? Is this love?" he asked.[6]

That evening, allowed to converse with the other condemned men and his gaolers, Martí spoke extensively about Sandino and the days he had spent in the Segovia mountains. He praised the general as one who had never given in to Yankee

6. Ibid, pp. 79-80.

imperialism. "Sandino," he said, "is one of the few patriots in the world." Their break had come, he went on, because Sandino was seeking aid from the Mexicans to resume the struggle in the Segovias, which Martí felt was hopeless and a waste of time. Further, Martí was already a communist in those days and Sandino rejected that doctrine.[7]

The next morning, Doña Nieves Cea de Zapata came again to say goodbye to her husband. According to the papers, "Her face was pallid, but serene." She did not cry as they embraced warmly and separated. No one came to say good-bye to Martí— his father was dead, his mother in Mexico City, and he was on bad terms with his other relatives. Nor did anyone visit Luna, whose mother and father were both dead, and whose family was in distant Ahuachapán, on the other side of the reign of terror. Zapata and Luna, firmly stating their faith in Catholicism, received the last sacraments from Fr. Castro Ramírez, who urged them to die "in communion with God." On hearing this word, Martí is said to have raised his eyes to heaven with a smile of bitter irony "and repeated the beautiful, and for him, meaningless, word God."[8]

His "confession" consisted of the impish trick of assuring his tormentors that there were still more than a thousand bombs planted in the city and that several thousand fresh rebels were waiting to rise in the capital. This no doubt had the effect of intensifying the persecution in San Salvador.

An ambulance waited at the gates of the fortress prison to convey them to the north wall of the general cemetery where they were to be executed by firing squad. It was this same vehicle which would wait to receive their bodies. They asked that Don Jacinto Castellanos Rivas be allowed to ride with them for company, and perhaps as a defense against the attentions of Fr. Prieto, who also insisted on riding in the crowded back of the ambulance, and who "did not abandon them for a moment."

The north wall of the cemetery is composed of huge blocks of stone, rising some fifteen feet. The cemetery has been built up behind this wall so that the graves are on a level with the top

7. Pineda, "Tragedia comunista," *Diario de Hoy*, February 7, 1967.
8. Jorge Schlesinger, *Revolución communista*, p. 198.

of the wall and high above the level of the street. Thus this wall of gigantic rock slabs is buttressed in turn by thousands of tons of dirt and the bones of the dead. Today the cemetery is surrounded by squalid, run-down neighborhoods, but in those days, when San Salvador was only a fifth of its present size, it stood near the edge of town. As there was no advance word of the execution, only a small crowd of the curious had collected by the time the procession of trucks and cars, the fatal ambulance among them, arrived. The chance spectators were kept back by a line of soldiers who descended from the trucks and took up positions at each end of the street to see to it that the execution was not disturbed.

As the prisoners were led to the wall, they passed General Eléazar López, the prosecutor at their trial. Luna stopped and said to him, "I pardon you for condemning me to death." Then he embraced him. The other two condemned men also gave the general an *abrazo* but said not a word. They then went to the wall and turned to face the firing squad. At the moment when the firing squad let fly its shots, another shot was said to have fallen into the crowd of officers; but, *Diario Latino* stated, "Happily, no one was hurt." The mysterious shot may have been imaginary, for although the real rebellion had been crushed, an almost superstitious terror of the communists remained.

The firing squad had run true to form—the prisoners were still alive after the discharge. An officer then went up and fired a shot into the heads of each of the men who lay writhing on the ground. The tension was now broken: the officers lit cigarettes and stood talking in hushed tones. Then someone noticed that Zapata was still bleeding profusely through the wound in his head, a sign that he was still alive some six or eight minutes after the first shots. They went up and shot him again, this time putting an end to the life of the young student.

The bodies were loaded into the ambulance and Fr. Prieto accompanied the dead as he had the living, back to the Central, where they lay until dispositions for the funerals, privately held, were arranged. After that, they were buried in the same cemetery, less than fifty yards from where they had fallen, in the raised area supported by the north wall. The graves of Luna and Zapata, which are still there, consist of slab tombs elevated about two feet above the level of the ground. On one tomb lies an open book in stone, to signify that it is the grave of a student; the other has ornate stone tracery. Martí was once beside them, but he was moved about 1968 to his mother's grave site which is down below in the section of the cemetery named in honor of Alberto Masferrer. His grave is now directly in back of the marble bust of Masferrer. At the time of my visit there were flowers around the statue of Masferrer, but none on the grave of Martí, perhaps because it is not yet properly marked. Those of Luna and Zapata, I was told by the caretaker, were frequently visited and often had fresh flowers placed on them.

Meantime, in the back country, the killings went on. It takes a while to kill ten thousand human beings. When burial proved impossible, and the stench from the roadsides grew too much to bear, the bodies of the dead were loaded on ox carts and taken to dumps, where they were covered with gasoline and burned. So Martí had in the end a relatively dignified death and was buried in the best bourgeois manner, while his followers died haphazardly and were received into common ash piles, as befitted proletarians.

No sooner was the revolt over than myths and legends about it began to grow. The government did nothing to retard this growth by its deliberate policy of silence on the subject. Government files were destroyed; the National Library was systematically purged of books and even newspapers concerning the revolt.[9]

One of the most persistent of the beliefs of the people of El Salvador concerning the events of 1932 is that hundreds of bourgeoisie were massacred in the course of the uprising. The belief has led to much permanent bitterness between the *campesinos* and the townsmen and to an abiding fear of the peasant majority. That is why strong units of *guardia*, armed with G.3 German automatic rifles, are stationed throughout the

9. I am told that this was done in the last days of the regime of Hernández Martínez, but it is noteworthy that no attempt has ever been made to build up material on the revolt. The National Library to this day has only the book by Joaquín Méndez, Jr.

countryside. But, as noted above, the actual number of deaths caused by the rebels was probably much smaller than generally imagined. If only two people were killed at Izalco, and two at Nahuizalco, three at Tacuba, and four at Juayúa, which were the major centers of the revolt, then it is hard to imagine that, altogether, more than thirty five civilians lost their lives. The revolt let loose an orgy of looting and burning, but not an orgy of rape and murder. Generally speaking, the peasants killed only when they were provoked or when they had some special grudge against a person. Rape also was committed, on occasion, but it was certainly the exception, not the rule. This study has also suggested that there were fewer *campesinos* killed than has popularly been believed, but with that calculation I am not on as firm a ground. Since one cannot recall the dead and have them pass in ghostly roll call before one, it is necessary to ask: What number seems most likely? The figure of ten thousand rings truer than higher estimates.

Another persistent belief in El Salvador is that the revolution was wholly manufactured by communists who received tremendous amounts of aid from abroad. The left, to counteract this, has often gone too far in the other direction, to the point of denying communist influence. In this case the truth does lie somewhere in between the two extremes (although historians are all too prone always to find it there). for there were real communists involved, some of whom, like Miguel Mármol, had even been to Russia. Propaganda and some small amounts of money were sent by Reds in New York. But the basic causes of the revolt had little to do with international Marxism. Rather, deep and abiding hostilities—economic, social, and cultural—lay at the base of the uprising. If these factors have been stressed in the present study, rather than communist influence, it is because they are in reality more important than the work of the small number of left-wing agitators who brought the crisis to a head.

Another point which must be clarified is the role of General Maximiliano Hernández Martínez in seizing power and in provoking the revolt. My interpretation, based on extensive conversations with persons involved, is that the general did not help plan the coup of December 2. Rather, he ostentatiously turned his back and ignored the planning which he felt might benefit him. He was probably genuinely taken by surprise when the coup occurred, not so much by the fact as by the timing; but like a good military man, he quickly made himself master of the situation. Again, in the case of the communist revolt, things simply broke his way. He could not order the communists to lead a revolt (though he did his best to annoy them at the time of the local elections), but he could only have been delighted that they proved foolish enough to revolt and to thus give him an opportunity to pose as the champion of law and order, not only to foreigners, but, more importantly, to the local wealthy class, whose support he desperately needed and was having a hard time winning.

It is to be hoped that something can be learned from these events concerning the dynamics of revolt in Latin America. The revolt came about because there was a framework of long-standing injustice and hatred, ready to be overlaid by a coating of propaganda. It came about because the normal tensions were increased through economic dislocation, making a barely tolerable situation completely unbearable in western El Salvador. Upon this, radicals, many of them real communists, were able to capitalize. Their revolt failed because they refused, or were unable, to take into account the fact that there were enough people—hostile or indifferent to the plight of the western, coffee-growing peasantry and aware of how much they had to lose if this *jacquerie* succeeded—to lend support to the government's policy of repression. One major difficulty may have been that Martí, for all his condescension toward the middle-class intellectuals Luna and Zapata, was himself a member of the landed aristocracy, and for this reason, or because of his long periods of exile, was not really in touch with the basic feelings of the Salvadorean man on the street. In any event, his long-hoped-for revolt was now over. The people, like the volcanos, ceased to rumble. The clouds of smoke from the towns of the western departments, like those from the mountaintops, dissipated and blew out over the clear, blue Pacific.

If, in his last hours, Martí had hoped that his revolt would at least receive some measure of praise from the communist world, he was doomed to disappointment. The *Communist,* the official monthly of the U.S. Communist party, while praising "the heroic struggles of the workers and peasants of Salvador, under the leadership of the Communist Party" as constituting "a landmark in the development of the revolutionary upsurge in the Caribbean countries and in the whole of Latin America," went on to denounce the uprising. It declared, "One of the chief lessons of the Salvadorean uprising is the danger of putchist and 'left' sectarian tendencies," and it blamed the leaders for not having prepared the masses for the struggle. Such are the virtues of hindsight.[10]

10. O. Rodríguez, "The Uprising in Salvador," *Communist* 11 (March 1932), pp. 248 and 251. The account of the revolt presented by this brief article is utterly fantastic.

Chapter 11

El Salvador since 1932

In mid-July, 1969, while most North Americans had their eyes glued to their television sets for the moon landing, I found myself bumping along a dirt road into occupied Honduras with the Salvadorean army. From time to time we passed tough, efficient-looking military patrols, armed with their superb G.3's that had done so much to make the lightning victory possible. Their looks showed that El Salvador was plainly on the move and would not rest until what she considered her national honor was salvaged. We cleared the road for an olive green column of armored personnel carriers that lumbered past toward the distant sound of small-arms fire. "See those," my companion said, "Those are made in El Salvador, from our own design. They were invented and built within three weeks, with sheet steel and regular truck bodies." There was an obvious note of national pride in his voice. The summer war of 1969 was plainly the biggest event in the nation's history since the *matanza*.

It made one realize how much things had changed in the space of thirty-seven years. And yet, many echoes of the revolt remain, many problems of that stormy period are yet unsolved. A question that must be asked by all thinking people in the country is: Will they be solved before an event more catastrophic than the revolt of 1932 occurs?

When the killing was over in March, 1932, the survivors, those who had hidden from the government-sponsored massacre, "meekly returned, much subdued."[1] There was much work to be done, much cleaning up. There were fields to be tilled,

1. Lilly de Jongh Osborne, *Four Keys to El Salvador* (New York: Funk, Inc., 1956) p. 184.

preparations to be made for next year's coffee harvest. The government turned from killing to conciliation and began to consider what should be done to prevent a repetition. Surprisingly thoughtful answers were often given. Joaquín Méndez, Jr., asked a number of persons about the problems of the country; one of them, Col. Marcelino Galdámez of Sonsonate, pointed out: "Communism is a tree shaken by the wind. The moving tree causes the seeds to fall; the same wind carries the seed to other places. The seed falls on fertile soil. To be done with communism it is necessary to make the ground sterile." How to do this was, of course, the problem. "In my view," said Santa Ana *político* J. Cipriano Castro, "the causes of the social crisis are...the economic depression...and the state of servitude in which our proletarian classes in the country live." To combat communism, he suggested legislation to protect the *campesino* and the worker. To José Tomás Calderón, the man in charge of putting down the revolt, the chief need was for education because ignorance was the thing which allowed radical agitation to flourish among the masses.[2]

General Martínez, who was no fool, realized that some improvements were necessary. To begin with, he sent out questionnaires through Salvador Castaneda Castro, his minister of *gobernación*, asking about land tenure, wages, and rations throughout the western provinces.[3] With this information he began to speculate on long-term reforms. Although he himself was no economist, he had the services of some shrewd men, most notably Miguel Tomás Molina, the former presidential candidate, and Napoleón Viera Altamirano. With hard-headed realism, these men set out to save the country from ruin.

The first measure was a negative one. El Salvador defaulted on her loan from the United States for $21 million, which had been contracted in 1922, and two days later all payments of foreign debts were temporarily suspended. The government further ordered that customs duties which had previously been given over to a representative of the American bankers, under terms of the 1922 loan, were to be paid directly

2. Méndez, *Sucesos comunistas*, pp. 18-19, 146, 198-99.
3. Ibid., pp. 136-38.

into the treasury of El Salvador. The bankers, of course, protested; but although the United States had not recognized Martínez, the State Department refused to come to their aid, perhaps because it did not want to embarrass the dictator who seemed the only bulwark against communism. Eventually terms were worked out for the resumption of interest payments in May, 1933.[4]

On March 12, 1932, a *ley moratoria* was passed, decreeing the suspension of payment of all domestic, private debts and a 40 percent reduction of the interest due on them.[5] This was to aid the coffee growers, whose plight was now desperate. The value of coffee had fallen to 57 percent of what it had been before the onset of the depression. Credit was the growers' most serious problem, next to the price itself, because it was almost always necessary to seek a loan to pay for the harvesting of the next crop. Three banks were chiefly responsible for the issuance of this credit. These giants were Banco Salvadoreño, the Banco Agrícola Comercial, and the Banco Ocidental. There was some credit to growers from the Banco Anglo-Sudamericano. The *ley moratoria* was aimed directly at these institutions, which also (in the case of the big three) issued their own paper money and speculated in foreign currency. Two years later, Martínez founded the Central Reserve Bank of El Salvador, chartered in June, 1934, as a private company but supported with government funds, and which operated in many ways like the Bank of England, whose advice had been sought in setting it up. The Banco Central de Reserva received the exclusive right to print money, to control the export and import of gold, and to control foreign exchange rates. The colón was pegged at 2.5 to the dollar, and there it has remained ever since, a remarkable example of fiscal stability.[6]

At the same time the Banco Hipotecario de El Salvador was founded to replace the big three as a lending institution for the coffee growers. This public institution could grant cheaper loans

4. Charles A. Thomson, "The Caribbean Situation: Nicaragua and Salvador," *Foreign Policy Reports* 9 (August 30, 1933), p. 148.
5. Marroquín, "Crisis," pp. 33-34.
6. Jorge Arias Gómez, "Informe verbal," in *El proceso político centroamericana* (San Salvador, 1964) p. 71.

and could lessen the burden of the coffee growers. To aid them further, the Coffee Growers Association was reorganized and the Compañía de Café was formed. The later institution became the chief marketer of Salvadorean coffee, a position it holds to this day. It buys from the *beneficios*, grades the coffee, thanks to the expert taste buds of Señor Joe Brown, and then markets the coffee overseas in Germany (for the better grades) and the United States.

As Abel Cuenca, among others, has objected, it might be that the effect of these measures was to shore up the foundations of the crumbling coffee culture and thus perpetuate the dead-end, one-crop economy of El Salvador.[7] This is certainly true, but at the time there was little or no industry in the country, and coffee, whether anyone approved or not, was the only thing that could be exchanged for foreign goods. Besides, a number of measures were undertaken that were not directly related to coffee. For instance, an association of cattle breeders came into existence. Farmers were urged to form cooperatives in the raising of cattle, cotton, corn, and other crops. Rural credit offices were set up to aid the small farmer and even a hesitant step was made toward land reform.

Such efforts came through the institution of Mejoramiento Social, an organization specifically designed to aid the *campesino*. Great estates were turned into Haciendas Nacionales and divided up. Roads were run between the small parcels, so that they could not be reunited, it was said. These Haciendas Nacionales came in for criticism on two grounds. Men of the left, such as Alejandro Dagoberto Marroquín, have pointed out that the land usually went to the dictator's personal friends, or to members of his Partido Pro-Patria. Further, less than 2 percent of the *campesinos* received land under this program. Joaquín Castro Canizales, from a more conservative point of view, attacks the program because the subdivision of the great estates caused the ruination of agriculture. After eye-witness examination of the Hacienda Santa Rosa and Hacienda Zapotitán, he reported that the woodlands had been destroyed,

7. Cuenca, *Democracia cafetalera*, pp. 33-34; Buezo, *Sangre de hermanos*, p. 106.

the great, pure-bred herds broken up, the production of grain disorganized. Further, despite the efforts of the government, neighboring estates were slowly buying up the best land, thus defeating the original intention of land reform.[8]

During all the reorganization, it should go without saying that Maximiliano Hernández Martínez kept himself in power. From his point of view, as has been noted, the communist uprising was a godsend. Our minister to Guatemala in 1932 even declared that the uprising had been "greatly exaggerated and used for political ends," and that Martínez was obtaining large sums of money from local capitalists so that he could continue his role as savior.[9]

Ultimately, however, the regime of the savior could not endure without U.S. recognition. Jefferson Caffery had created a strong false impression that recognition would be forthcoming, but the State Department said otherwise and insisted that our treaty obligations prevented recognition of an illegally constituted government. Martínez was thus forced to hunt for a pseudo-successor who could turn over authority to himself again after a suitable lapse of time. His first thought was of Col. José Asencio Menéndez, who was on his way home from a tour of duty in Paris when the revolt occurred. This suggestion was opposed by the military. Besides, Rodolfo Duke, still playing kingmaker, wanted Menéndez, and that may have turned the dictator against him, for Martínez planned to break the power of the "big three" banks. Instead he chose Fidel Cristino Garay, another colonel, as "first designate" for succession. This prompted Osmín Aguirre to threaten revolt rather than serve under Garay; although Aguirre was then removed as police chief on April 13, 1932, Garay was later replaced by the more

8. Quino Caso, "Acontecimientos," *Tribuna Libre*, January 30 and Feburary 5, 1952; Marroquín, "Crisis," p. 35. This land reform program functioned chiefly between 1933 and 1937. Coffee lands were not touched as everyone realized that this would be disastrous.
9. N.A., R.G. 59, Whitehouse to Secretary of State, February 8, 1932, file 816.00/842. William J. McCafferty, chargé in San Salvador, denied that the revolt was exaggerated (ibid., January 21, file 816.00/844).

respectable General Andrés Ignacio Menéndez, a man of upright character and liberal sentiments.[10]

The general actually became provisional president in August, 1934, making Martínez his minister of war. Then elections were held in March of 1935 in which only the former dictator's Partido Pro-Patria saw fit to participate. Martínez, being the only candidate, was made president again; the forms having been observed, the United States promptly extended to him the coveted recognition. The truth was that almost everyone agreed that Martínez had done a good job and that no one else could handle the situation. Even during the few months of Menéndez's presidency there was a new "communist conspiracy" uncovered, a circumstance which must have resigned many persons of influence to the return of the savior.

Whether recognized as legal or not, the regime was, after 1935, a thorough-going police state, and Martínez, who dabbled more and more in spiritualism and the occult, appeared less competent than before, now that he was fully entrenched. One cause of difficulties was the sudden increase in population; another was the shift of the population from the countryside to the city, which was now in full swing. Because of the numerical growth, even with people leaving the land there remained more on the farms than could be fed or employed, while in the city there was little work for the newcomers. Shack towns, still the bane of San Salvador, began to appear.

World War II brought a return of prosperity, but as the new boom was in industry rather than coffee, the industrialists became increasingly annoyed at a regime which still looked to coffee for the wealth of the country. Thus pressures built up— even the radicals reappeared. Old-style communist Miguel Mármol worked behind the scenes and the young radicals found a leader in Alejandro D. Marroquín.

More moderate dissent crystalized around Arturo Romero and the interim president Andrés I. Menéndez. The Romeristas, as they were called, resorted in 1944 to a general strike to bring down the government, but Martínez met them with repression.

10. N.A., R.G. 59, McCafferty to Secretary of State, January 18, 1932, file 816.00/825; see also files 816.00/865 and /866.

As long as the army held firm, the dictator was able to weather the storm. He drowned in blood an uprising of the university students. But strong pressures from the United States, and finally a lack of support from his close military associates, caused Martínez to flee into exile, and a provisional government was set up. The former dictator never returned. He died in Honduras in 1966, murdered, in a labor dispute, by a workman on his hacienda.

The new junta, headed by Andrés I. Menéndez, had visions of a democratic El Salvador. That included, of necessity, allowing opposition to flourish, which also meant allowing the communists to reorganize. But the military men watched all this with growing alarm, especially as a radical labor union, the Unión Nacional de Trabajadores, gained strength, growing to fifty thousand members by October, 1944.[11]

The forces of reaction then discovered their leader in Colonel Osmín Aguirre y Salinas, the former dictator's one-time police chief. With the backing of the higher military officers, Aguirre staged a coup on October 21, 1944. The liberal regime collapsed with distressing ease and the tough policeman installed himself as provisional president, beginning what Arias Gómez has styled "a reign of terror." Whether one wants to call it that or not, it can be said with certainty that Osmín Aguirre cracked down on the UNT and the communists. He drove even the liberal leaders into exile, where they formed a government under Miguel Tomás Molina, a long-time *político* who had been an architect of Martínez's reforms in the mid-thirties. An attempted uprising against the conservative regime in the suburb of San Miguelito was crushed on December 8, and a liberal invasion from Guatemala (such as Araujo had once dreamed of making) was crushed four days later.[12]

Aguirre was the personification of the coffee-grower interests. But he was not without popular support. In Izalco, for instance, the Indian cacique Félix Turish supported him against the Ladinos of the town who were mostly Romeristas.

11. Alexander, *Communism*, pp. 369-70; Osborne, *El Salvador*, p. 58.
12. Alexander, *Communism*, pp. 370-71; Arias Gómez, "Informe verbal," p. 72.

Aguirre went through with the elections which had been promised by the ousted liberals, but he made sure that the coffee candidate, General Salvador Casteñeda Castro, won these elections. After he took office on March 5, 1945, General Casteñeda Castro continued the purge begun by the provisional government, driving most of the radicals out of the country for good. After a while the regime found it possible (and expedient, as its base of support was quite weak), to allow greater freedom. Constitutional normality appeared to be returning. Economically, however, the attempt of the regime to go back to the good old days of coffee culture did not prove entirely successful. Industrial expansion was harmed and coffee prices failed to rise sufficiently to justify government policies. Toward the close of his legitimate term, the general began efforts to prolong his period in office, having his eye on the example of the last general to be president of the country. If, like Martínez, Casteneda Castro had managed to appear as a savior, he might have turned the trick, but conditions were unfavorable. A liberal regime existed in neighboring Guatemala. Coffee prices took a downward turn and the masses were restless. Faced with the prospect of another long dictatorship, the younger army officers decided to act.[13]

The "Majors' coup" of December 14, 1948, was the result. These younger officers, headed by Oscar Osorio (who defeated José Asencio Menéndez for the presidency in a 1950 election marked by charges of fraud), talked reform and in truth did a good deal. They allowed industrial workers to organize again, but refused the same right to *campesinos*. They founded a social security system and tried to reorganize the ramshackle bureaucracy. Toward that end they brought in a private consulting firm from the United States for a general administrative survey. This was followed by a period of revamping and training of personnel, and the administration of El Salvador was vastly improved.

Growing resistance by the wealthy, particularly the coffee oligarchy, cut down the reform tendencies of the young officers,

13. Cuenca, *Democracia cafetalera*, p. 35; Arias Gómez, "Informe verbal," p. 73.

especially after Lt. Col. Osorio had served out his term as president and turned the government over to José María Lemus. Lemus proved a harsh and dictatorial man, noted chiefly for his political persecutions, of which perhaps the most famous was that of Roberto Edmundo Canessa, former head of the Cafetalera. A former minister of justice and playboy diplomat, he was beaten in prison and died shortly after being released.

Surrounded by increasingly vocal opposition both in the civilian and military sectors, Lemus, like Martínez before him, turned his exasperation on the university: he ordered his *guardia* to invade, and a number of students were injured. Shortly after this incident, Lemus was turned out by a coup on October 26, 1960. He fled into exile and a reform junta took over.

But it seemed like 1944 all over again. The reform leaders proved entirely too radical for the army officers and oligarchs. A revived Confederación General de Trabajadores Salvadoreños began to flourish. Certain junta leaders began to be accused of looking to Castro's Cuba for support. When the Junta de Gobierno went so far as to threaten to hold really free elections, the military decided that it was time to restore law and order. The restoration took the form of a *cuartelazo* led by the Colonels Aníbal Portillo and Julio Rivera. They did not succeed in making their coup bloodless. The citizens in San Salvador tried to hold on to their newly won freedom, and eighty persons were killed in clashes with the *guardia*.[14]

The coup of January 25, 1961 is the most recent in the history of El Salvador. It brought into power the presently reigning system. For a year and a half, the two colonels ran the country through a military junta. To the rich they offered the choice of reform or another left-wing revolt, and they succeeded in putting through a number of rather mild measures—mild, that is, compared to what the country really needed. These included an obligatory day of rest for the peasants on the *fincas* and *haciendas*, the nationalization of the Central Reserve Bank of El Salvador, rent reduction, an export and exchange control law,

14. De la Selva, "Lucha," pp. 215-19; Arias Gómez, "Informe verbal," p. 75; Edwin Lieuwen, *Generals versus Presidents* (New York, Washington and London: Praeger Inc., 1964), p. 92.

and a timid agrarian reform, based on conservation and better land use rather than expropriation.[15]

When they took over in 1961, .01 percent of the landholders owned 16 percent of the land. Their estates covered at least 2,500 acres each. Some 85 percent of the farmers owned 12.4 acres or less. The rich landholders, many of them coffee growers, have given rise to the legend of the "fourteen families" who are said to control the country. In fact, an interrelated oligarchy of about a hundred major families really run El Salvador. Some of these are newcomers, some even Turcos, but many have been prominent for a century or more. If the power of the oligarchy was really to be touched, more radical measures were necessary. In fact, in many ways, the laws to protect the *campesino* have backfired. Since the coup of 1961 a minimum wage law has been put into effect, but all that this has meant for the coffee workers is that the landholders pay slightly more and no longer give the customary two free meals of tortillas and beans each day. Thus the worker's total wages have declined.

In 1961 elections were held for a constituent assembly to draft a new constitution for El Salvador. Only the official party, the Party of National Conciliation (PCN), won any seats in this body, which then drafted a "democratic" constitution for the country. Presidential elections were held in April, 1962, and again only the PCN participated. Julio Rivera became legal president of the country. Nor did the democratically elected president have much trouble with his unicameral legislature, for only the PCN had any seats. In justice to Rivera, it should be noted that he soon moved to remedy this situation. A proportional representation law was passed in 1963 which made it possible for opposition parties to win twenty seats out of fifty-two in the 1964 elections. By 1968 opposition groups held almost half the seats in the unicameral. Further, the colonel attempted social reforms, with an income tax law and new labor

15. De la Selva, "Lucha," p. 218.

legislation, but unfortunately, strong opposition from the oligarchy caused a slowdown of social reform after 1964.[16]

When the five-year presidential term was drawing to a close in late 1966, it was decided that presidential elections would also be made more open. Nonofficial parties were encouraged not to boycott the presidential election, and as a result there were three major candidates: the official candidate, Col. Fidel Sánchez Hernández; Dr. Abraham Rodríguez, representing the fast-surging Christian Democratic Party (PDC); and the tall, handsome rector of the University of El Salvador, Dr. Fabio Castillo of the Party of Renovating Action (PAR), a group from the radical, but not necessarily communist, left. It was no surprise to anyone that the official candidate won the March, 1967, election, but the degree of freedom in the elections was surprising, despite some use of intimidation and Red-scare techniques against the PAR. It was the closest approach the country had made to democracy since 1931.

President Sánchez Henández, a round-faced, short man with a Nixon-like five o'clock shadow, proved in many ways more dynamic than his predecessor. He tried to start reform rolling again after the three-year dead period from 1964 to 1967. However, he ran into a number of difficulties. One problem was the growing militancy of El Salvador's overworked and underpaid teachers. Their union launched a strike in February, 1968, which soon threatened to become a revolution. Most other unions went out in support of the teachers. Even parents' groups were formed to boycott those schools which stayed open. Eventually the issue was settled on terms favorable to the teachers, but it was a close call for the president. Another difficulty was the growing tension with Honduras over the three hundred thousand Salvadoreños who have migrated there from their own overcrowded country. López Arellano, the Honduran strongman president, in deep economic trouble at home, decided to take his people's minds off their problems by an

16. Lieuwen, *Generals versus Presidents*, p. 93, Harry Kantor, "El Salvador: The Military as Reformists," in *Patterns of Politics and Political Systems in Latin America* (Chicago: Rand McNally, 1969), p. 125. Kantor says that the existence of opposition members in the legislature has "put more life" into politics.

anti-Salvadorean campaign. Tensions increased in 1968 when a patrol from El Salvador was captured near the disputed border.

Although the situation at that time was tense, no one thought that it would lead to war. But in the Honduran province of Olancho, a gang of thugs called the Mancha Brava began a sporadic campaign of terrorism against settlers from El Salvador. Tensions slowly increased and there was bitter feeling by the time of the Central American soccer championship matches, a part of the World Cup competition, which pitted Honduras against El Salvador in May and June, 1969. After the second match was won by El Salvador, large numbers of refugees began to tumble back across the border. Whether they were actually being pursued by Honduran terrorists or whether it was simply a case of mass hysteria is a debatable question, but their plight was a real one. By early July there were some fifteen thousand of these poor people in El Salvador and the prospect of more on the way.

El Salvador broke diplomatic relations with Honduras on June 27, but the surprise Salvadorean attack, "just like Israel's," as they said, caught diplomatic observers off guard. The attack was launched on July 14 and quickly gobbled up a good deal of Honduran territory. After a week of fighting, the Organization of American States arranged a cease-fire, and, after much arm twisting, persuaded El Salvador to withdraw without any real guarantees of better treatment for her citizens in Honduras. President Sánchez Hernández claimed a great victory for his diplomacy as well as his arms and held a parade through the capital. It had indeed been a military victory, and it had taken people's minds off domestic problems.

In the early days, Rivera and the PCN were hailed as a progressive force. John F. Kennedy said that "governments of the civil-military type of El Salvador are the most effective in containing communist penetration in Latin America."[17] And in 1964 the distinguished American student of Latin American politics Edwin Lieuwen declared, "Here is the only country in Latin America in which the armed forces organization is both

17. De La Selva, "Lucha," p. 217.

leading and supporting the nation along the pathways of democratic, evolutionary, social revolution."[18] But the PCN now seems to be running out of steam. Other political forces are present. Perhaps the most popular politicians in 1969 were Fabio Castillo, who tried to start a Revolutionary party, and José Napoleón Duarte, the dynamic PDC mayor of San Salvador. But as long as the army, and the National Guard of "Chele" Medrano, back the PCN, it will probably stay in power.

The truth is that, whoever is in power, the basic problem of the country remains insoluble: population is outrunning development. During the early sixties there was a boom in El Salvador. With Japanese aid, cotton production was increased and textile mills were set up. A number of other industries, such as coffee processing, cement, vegetable oil processing, and even a small steel plant for processing scrap, were set up.[19] But cotton has not been doing as well as expected, the boom has tapered off, and a mood of disillusionment has set in. Meanwhile the population continues to grow. In 1961, when there were some 2,500,000 souls in the country, statisticians projected a growth rate of 3 percent per year. If 1969 estimates of 3,260,000 people in the country are correct, that projection was about fulfilled. Per capita income is almost static at $245.00 per year.

There are many reasons why population continues to rise. Salvadorean concepts of virility are linked to fertility. It is a country where many people will not eat unfertilized eggs nor sow hybrid corn in the fields for fear of sterility. Also, there is a resentment in El Salvador, as among the Negro community in the United States, because it appears to the people that the gringos want to reduce their numbers so that they will have fewer people to aid. Further, the intransigent attitude of Pope Paul VI has not aided birth control. All this is a great pity,

18. Lieuwen, *Generals versus Presidents*, p. 92.
19. Raynolds, *Rapid Development*, pp. 37-43. His prediction that "the industrial expansion which lies ahead in the next few years will probably be more rapid, yet more difficult, than the initial efforts of the last three decades" (p. 55) has proved true regarding the difficulty, but false regarding the rapid expansion.

because if something is not done soon, a terrible fate awaits El Salvador and other such nations. It is unrealistic to assume that the growth rate could ever overtake the current birth rate.

Ironically enough, while the per capita income of $245.00 does not seem to be increasing very rapidly, one notes a growing middle class in the country. Walking through the miles of San Salvador suburbs around Colonia Escalón and San Benito one might seem to be in San Diego or Miami. There are neat, not overly large, well-kept houses, with a car in every garage. But it is illusory to think of these people in United States terms. An aristocratic standard still prevails, and if a man becomes successful in business the thing that he wishes most is to buy a *finca* or a *hacienda* so that his son will be a gentleman and not be tied to the sordid world of business. And there are enough skeleton-like old Indian women shuffling through the streets of San Benito begging alms or selling spoiled fruit so that one is aware one is not in San Diego.

El Salvador is still dependent on coffee, and even if coffee were not the mainstay of the economy, the chances are that it would be replaced by cotton, sugar, or some other crop, rather than industry. Only a complete revolution in population control, national goals, and land use could drastically change El Salvador; it is hard to imagine the PCN, which is closely tied to the old order, creating such a revolution.

El Salvador's leaders like to think of their political and social system as comparable to that of Mexico, also a state with one dominant political party which considers itself an agent of progress and change. But the truth is that what El Salvador wants is to enjoy the benefits of the Mexican Revolution without first having that cataclysmic social overturn which was the Mexican Revolution. This might be possible, but difficult to accomplish. It may well be that the ghosts of 1932 will yet return to haunt the country.

In reality, they have haunted the country all along. Memories of the uprising account for the almost paranoiac fear of communism that has gripped the nation ever since. This fear is expressed in the continual labeling of even the most modest reform movements as communist or communist inspired. It is perhaps best expressed in the fact that since 1932 every president or chief of state of the country has been a military man. Indeed, the whole political labyrinth of El Salvador can be explained only in reference to the traumatic experience of the uprising and the *matanza*.[20]

Like most ghosts, the specter of 1932 prospers best in twilight and shadow. For this reason, the ruling military powers have deliberately tried to keep the true nature of the events of that year from the people. They have fostered a legend of bloodthirsty mobs butchering thousands of middle-class citizens, and of a heroic army that barely managed to turn back the barbarian wave. Little has been written on the revolt, except propaganda. The National Library has been purged even of the newspapers that cover the period of the revolt. Government files have been conveniently "lost."

And yet, the old order cannot last forever. Some day more serious reformers than the colonels will come along and gain control of the country. When that day comes, El Salvador will be able to reevaluate the events of the thirties.

In El Salvador, the two men with the most statues, monuments, and edifices named in their honor are Gerardo Barrios, whom Salvadoreans shot, and Alberto Masferrer, whom they exiled. No doubt, in time, Agustín Farabundo Martí will have his statues and schools too, and will be remembered as a champion of the poor against the rich, a colorful character of a distant revolutionary epoch. But by that time El Salvador will differ as much from the El Salvador of today as the country today differs from the slumbering, backward land where a few determined men provoked the great peasant uprising of 1932.

20. For an extended discussion of this point, see Stephen L. Rozman, "The Socialization of Military Rule in El Salvador" (Paper presented at the Rocky Mountain Social Science Convention, May, 1970).

Bibliography

PRINTED WORKS

Adams, Richard N. *Cultural Surveys of Panama, Nicaragua, Guatemala, El Salvador, and Honduras.* Washington: Pan American Sanitary Bureau, 1957.

Alba, Pedro de. "La educación vitalista de Alberto Masferrer." *Cuadernos Americanos* 3 (1945): 233-60.

Alba, Víctor. *Historia del comunismo en América Latina.* Mexico, 1954.

Alemán Bolaños, G. *Sandino!* San Salvador, 1932.

Alexander, Robert J. *Communism in Latin America.* New Brunswick, N.J.: Rutgers University Press, 1957.

Anderson, Charles W. "El Salvador: The Army as Reformer." In *Political Systems of Latin America,* ed. by Martin C. Needler, pp. 53-72. Princeton, N.J.: Van Nostrand, 1964.

[Arias Goméz, Jorge.] *Biografía de Agustín Farabundo Martí.* San Salvador, 1967.

"Informe verbal." In *El Proceso político centroamericano,* pp. 67-77. San Salvador, 1964.

Barón Castro, Rodolfo. *La población de El Salvador: Estudio acerca de su desvolvimiento desde la época prehispánica hasta nuestros días.* Madrid, 1942.

Buezo, Rodolfo. *Sangre de hermanos.* Havana, n.d.

Bustamante Maceo, Gregorio. *Historia militar de El Salvador.* San Salvador, 1951.

Caffery, Jefferson, and Matthews, Freeman. "State Department Press Release." Mimeographed. Washington, D.C.: Department of State, December 19, 1931.

Calderón, Gen. José Tomás. *Breve reseña histórica del comunismo en El Salvador.* San Salvador, 1932.

— "Población-tierra-trabajo." *Revista del Ateneo de El Salvador,* no. 145 (1932): 8-10.

— *Sufragio libre: 8 de diciembre de 1929.* San Salvador, 1931.

Calderón, Col. Julio César. *Episodios nacionales: El indio Anastasio Aquino en Santiago Nonualco en 1833 y causa de su rebelión.* San Salvador, 1957.

Castro Canizales, Joaquín [Quino Caso]. "Acontecimientos de enero de 1932," *Tribuna Libre*, January-February, 1952.

Contreras, Juan José. *Monografía de la población indígena de Nahuizalco*. San Salvador, 1963.

Contreras Castro, Julio. *De como fue traicionado El Presidente Ingeniero Arturo Araujo por Maximiliano Hernández Martínez*. San Salvador, 1944.

Cuenca, Abel. *El Salvador: Una democracia cafetalera*. San Salvador, n.d.

Domínguez Sosa, Julio Alberto. *Ensayo histórico sobre las tribus Nonualcas y su caudillo Anastasio Aquino*. San Salvador, 1964.

Durand, Mercedes. "Entrevista con el ex-presidente Don Arturo Araujo." *Diario Latino*, January 5, 1968.

Ekholm, Gordon F., and Willey, Gordon R., eds. *Handbook of Middle American Indians: Archeological Frontiers and External Connections, Vol. 4*. Austin, Texas: University of Texas Press, 1966.

Flakoll, Darwin J., and Alegría, Claribel. *Cenizas de Izalco*. Barcelona, 1966. [Novel.] *Ashes of Izalco*, translated by Darwin J. Flakoll. Willimantic, CT: Curbstone Press, 1989.

"'Fusilado' relata episodio de 1932." *Diario de Hoy*, May 11, 1969.

Government of El Salvador. Ministerio de Relaciones Exteriores. *El gobierno del Presidente Gral: Maximiliano Hernández Martínez ante la constitución política de El Salvador y el tratado de paz y amistad suscrito por las Repúblicas de Centro America....diversas opiniones*. San Salvador, 1932.

Hackett, Charles W. "Communist Uprising in El Salvador." *Current History* 35 (March, 1932): 843-44.

Herrera Vega, Adolfo. *El indio occidental de El Salvador y su incorporación social por la escuela*. Izalco, El Salvador, 1935.

Kantor, Harry. "El Salvador: The Military as Reformists." In *Patterns of Politics and Political Systems in Latin America*, pp. 107-29. Chicago: Rand McNally, 1969.

Karnes, Thomas L. *The Failure of Union: Central America, 1824-1960*. Chapel Hill, N.C.: University of North Carolina Press, 1961.

Lieuwen, Edwin. *Generals versus Presidents*. New York, Washington and London: Praeger Inc., 1964.

López Vallecillos, Italo. *El periodismo en El Salvador: Bosquejo histórico-documental....* San Salvador, 1964.

Luna, David Alejandro. "Algunas facetas sociales en la vida de Agustín Farabundo Martí." *Revista Salvadoreña de Ciencias Sociales* 1 (January-March 1965): 89-108.

— "Un heroico y trágico suceso de nuestra historia." In *El proceso político centroamericano*, pp. 49-65. San Salvador, 1964.

Macaulay, Neill. *The Sandino Affair.* Chicago: Quadrangle Books Inc., 1967.

Machón Vilanova, Francisco. *Ola roja.* Mexico, 1948. [Novel.]

Martz, John D. *Central America: The Crisis and the Challenge.* Chapel Hill, N.C.: University of North Carolina Press, 1959.

Masferrer, Alberto. *Cartas a un obrero.* San Salvador, n.d.

— *El dinero maldito.* San Salvador, n.d.

— *El minimun vital.* San Salvador, n.d.

Masferrer C., Manuel. *Vida anecdótica de Alberto Masferrer.* San Salvador, 1957.

Méndez, Joaquín, Jr. *Los sucesos comunistas en El Salvador.* San Salvador, 1932.

Mendieta Alfaro, Roger. *¿Democracia o comunismo?* San Salvador, n.d.

Mestas, Alberto de. *El Salvador: Pais de lagosy volcanos.* Madrid, 1950.

Meza Gallont, Rafael. *El éjercito de El Salvador: Breve boceto historico.* San Salvador, 1964.

Ministerio de Educación. *En torno a Masferrer.* San Salvador, 1956.

Osborne, Lilly de Jongh. *Four Keys to El Salvador.* New York: Funk, Inc., 1956.

Osegueda, Francisco R. "Observaciones sobre la vida del campesino salvadoreño de otros tiempos y la del campesino actual." *Revista del Ateneo de El Salvador*, no. 145 (1932) 11-15.

Paredes, Jacinto. *Vida y obras del Dr. Pío Romero Bosque: Apuntes para la historia de El Salvador.* San Salvador, 1930.

Parker, F. D. *The Central American Republics.* London: Royal Institute of International Affairs, 1964.

Pena Trejo, Gen. Salvador. "Narracion historica de la insurreccion militar de 2 de diciembre de 1931." *Diario Latino*, April-June, 1964.

Pineda, Gustavo [and others]. "La tragedia comunista de 1932." *Diario de Hoy*, January-March, 1967.

Poblete Troncoso, Moisés, and Burnett, Ben G. *The Rise of the Latin American Labor Movement.* New Haven, CT.: Yale University Press, 1960.

Poppino, Rollie E. *International Communism in Latin America: A History of the Movement, 1917-1963.* New York: Free Press, 1964.

Raynolds, David R. *Rapid Development in Small Economies: The Example of El Salvador*. New York, Washington and London: Praeger Inc., 1967.

Rodríguez, Mario. *Central America*. Englewood Cliffs, N.J.: Prentice Hall, 1965.

Rodriguez, O. "The Uprising in Salvador." *Communist* 11 (March, 1932): 248-51.

Schlesinger, Alfredo. *La verdad sobre el comunismo*. 2d ed. Guatemala, 1932.

Schlesinger, Jorge. *Revolución comunista*. Guatemala, 1946.

Selva, Mauricio de la. "El Salvador: Tres décadas de lucha." *Cuadernos Americanos* 21 (January-February, 1962): 196-220.

Silva, Lautaro. *La herida roja de América*. Vol. 2. Ciudad Trujillo, 1959.

Smith, T. Lynn. "Notes on the Population and Rural Social Organization in El Salvador." *Rural Sociology* 10 (1945): 359-79.

Thomson, Charles A. "The Caribbean Situation: Nicaragua and Salvador." *Foreign Policy Reports* 9 (August 30, 1933): 142-48.

U.S. Department of State. *Foreign Relations of the United States: The American Republics*. Vol. 5. Washington, D.C.: Government Printing Office, 1948.

MANUSCRIPTS

Aguirre y Salinas, Osmín. "Los Sucesos de enero de 1932." In the possession of Thomas P. Anderson.

Calderón, Col. Julio C. "Memorial histórico: Lo que no se dijo de la rebelión comunista en Ahuachapán, Sonsonate y Santa Ana en el año 1932." In the possession of Sr. Miguel Pinto, Jr.

Castro Canizales, Joaquín [Quino Caso]. "Narración histórica de la insurrección militar del 2 de diciembre de 1931: Acotaciones, aclaraciones, y rectificaciones al estudio del General Salvador Peña Trejo." In the possession of Sr. Castro.

Elam, Robert Varney. "Appeal to Arms: The Army and Politics in El Salvador, 1931-1964." Ph.D. dissertation, University of New Mexico, 1968.

Marroquín, Alejandro D. "Estudio sobre la crisis de los años treinta en El Salvador." In the possession of Dr. Marroquín.

Rozman, Stephen L. "The Socialization of Military Rule in El Salvador." Paper presented at the Rocky Mountain Social Science Convention, May, 1970.

Wilson, Everett A. "The Crisis of National Integration in El Salvador, 1919-1935." Ph.D. dissertation, Stanford University, 1970.

NEWSPAPERS (All San Salvador)

Of 1930-32:
Diario Latino
Diario del Salvador
Estrella Roja
Opinión Estudiantil
Patria
La Prensa
Verdad

Later Newspapers:
Diario de Hoy
Tribuna Libre

DOCUMENTS

National Archives, Washington, D.C. Record Group 59. Series 816.00, El Salvador, 1920-32, and related documents.

Osmín Aguirre Collection (documents in his personal files):
Manifesto of Federación Juvenil Comunista, August, 1931.
Letter to Central Committee of Communist Party from Julio Galves, January 1, 1932.
Letter by Director of Central Penitentiary on Martí, January 19, 1932.
Letter to Central Committee of Communist Party from R. Gómez, January 23, 1932.
Receipt for prisoners, January 24, 1932.
Letter from Fiscal Militar to director of the Polícia, January 27, 1932.
Letter from Captain Herrera on communists captured, January 30,
Telegram from Castañeda on capture of communists, January 30, 1932.
Letter from A. C. Bendeke to Neftali Lagos, Usulutan, March 18, 1932.
Document of Ministerio de Gobernación on communist propaganda, 1932.
Message on Araujo from Joaquín G. Valencia.

INTERVIEWS

(As more than a hundred persons were consulted, only the more important ones are listed here.)

Abarca, José elderly *campesino* of Nahuizalco who witnessed revolt.

Aguirre y Salinas, Osmín, head of the National Police at the time of the revolt (interview conducted by means of notes).

Arias Gómez, Jorge, university professor, biographer of Martí.

Barillas Calderón, Dr. Carlos, classmate of Mario Zapata.

Block, Pablo, coffee dealer in Sonsonate during the period of the revolt.

Calvo, Alfredo, historian of Izalco.

Cardona, Rubén, landholder near Nahuizalco at the time of the revolt.

Castro Canizales, Joaquín, journalist, leader of the 1931 coup.

Cuenca, Abel, leader of the communist movement in Tacuba in 1932.

Díaz Barrientos, Alfonso, citizen who resisted rebels in Izalco during the revolt.

Geoffroy Rivas, Pedro, official of the Ministerio de Hacienda, associate of many of the leaders of the 1932 revolt.

Granadino, J. Hugo, boy in Nahuizalco at the time of the revolt, now a historian living in Sonsonate.

Herrera, José Roberto, *alcalde* of Izalco in 1969. Eighteen years old at time of revolt, he joined the Civic Guard.

Luna, Dr. David Alejandro, university historian. No relation to Alfonso Luna.

Marroquín, Dr. Alejandro D., university professor who knew Luna and Zapata at the university. He is a leading authority on modern El Salvador.

Mendoza, José Raúl, telegraphist of Ahuachapán in 1932. He was secretary of the special court set up to try the rebels. He had been a boyhood friend of Alfonso Luna.

Menéndez, José Asencio, deputy minister of defense in 1932, organizer of the Civic Guard.

Olivo, Juan José, *alcalde* of Juayúa in 1969, fifteen years old at the time of the revolt. His father led the town band which was forced to play for the rebels.

Orellana, Prof. Carlos, schoolmaster of Izalco during the revolt. He is the author of a local history of Sonsonate.

Orosco, Francisco Xavier, citizen of Izalco, served in the army during the revolt.

Padilla Velasco, René, official of the Foreign Ministry, the legal advisor of Martí, Luna, and Zapata at the January, 1932, trial.

Peña Trejo, Gen. Salvador, commandant of the Escuela Militar and leader of the Civic Guard in Ahuachapán during the 1932 revolt.

Pinto, Miguel, Jr., director of *Diario Latino*, who remembers Martí during 1931.

Quiteño, Serafín, journalist from a landholding family of Izalco.

Shupan, Eulalio, elderly Indian *campesino* of Izalco, grandson of Patricio Shupan.

Sol Castellanos, Dr. Jorge, one of El Salvador's leading economists.

Turish, Félix, cacique of Izalco in 1969, who was Feliciano Ama's chief assistant before the 1932 revolt.

Index